THE TOMBSTONE COOKBOOK

RECIPES AND LORE FROM THE TOWN TOO TOUGH TO DIE

SHERRY MONAHAN

TWODOT®

GUILFORD, CONNECTICUT
HELENA, MONTANA

A · TWODOT® · BOOK

An imprint of Globe Pequot, the trade division of
The Rowman & Littlefield Publishing Group, Inc.
4501 Forbes Blvd., Ste. 200
Lanham, MD 20706
www.rowman.com

Distributed by NATIONAL BOOK NETWORK

British Library Cataloguing in Publication Information available

Library of Congress Cataloging-in-Publication Data
Names: Monahan, Sherry, author.
Title: The Tombstone cookbook : recipes and lore from the town too tough to die / Sherry Monahan.
Description: Guilford, Connecticut : TwoDot, [2022] | Includes index. | Summary: "Features more than 120 recipes inspired by Tombstone's historic eateries and adapted for the modern home cook, as well as information about the region's history and lore through sidebars and historic photos"— Provided by publisher.
Identifiers: LCCN 2021031911 (print) | LCCN 2021031912 (ebook) | ISBN 9781493053865 (paperback) | ISBN 9781493053872 (electronic)
Subjects: LCSH: Cooking, American—Arizona—Tombstone. | LCGFT: Cookbooks.
Classification: LCC TX909 .M566 2022 (print) | LCC TX909 (ebook) | DDC 641.59791/53—dc23
LC record available at https://lccn.loc.gov/2021031911
LC ebook record available at https://lccn.loc.gov/2021031912

♾™ The paper used in this publication meets the minimum requirements of American National Standard for Information Sciences—Permanence of Paper for Printed Library Materials, ANSI/NISO Z39.48-1992.

To Larry, for supporting my author dreams

CONTENTS

PREFACE

This is my second foray into the cuisine of Tombstone. In 2008 I collected 140 recipes and the history of the town in a book called *Taste of Tombstone*. A lot has changed since then, but how I became enamored with Tombstone hasn't.

I still tell people that my love affair began the first time I saw it back in the 1990s. I remember the day as if it was last week when we drove down Allen Street (back when you still could) and parked our white rental car. I opened the door and planted my cowboy boots on the wooden boardwalk. It was magical, and I felt like I had transcended time—that I had been there before, or even lived there in another lifetime.

Random thoughts filled my mind as I strolled the boardwalks in this historic town. I wondered what it was like to live in Tombstone back in the 1880s. What kind of place was it? What did the townspeople do for fun? What type of food was served when Wyatt Earp and Doc Holliday lived there? Where did they eat? Who owned and ran the restaurants and other food establishments in town? On the plane ride home, I decided I wanted to be connected to Tombstone, and a recipe formed in my head. I blended my passion for writing, history, and cooking, and the first book was published.

This cookbook includes some of those details, but this is a new book with new details, recipes, stories, and photos. Interesting historical details are woven around recipes to offer a sense of what it was like to live back in a time when cowboys, miners, mixologists, and townspeople enjoyed a first-class dining experience with silver, china, and linen in tents and buildings.

Thanks to all those who helped test recipes and voted on photos, and to my editor and our team for making this book awesome.

Sherry Monahan

INTRODUCTION

TOMBSTONE, ARIZONA, IS A TOWN THAT WAS FORMED because of the silver mines that produced tons of ore in the 1880s. In its heyday, residents and guests had elegant hotels and restaurants, trendy imported goods, and everything in between. Before delving into the recipes, let's explore some of the town's history.

Before silver was discovered, Tombstone was nothing more than a vast expanse of high desert where Cochise and the Chiricahua Apache sometimes roamed. The only Anglo civilization in the area was found on remote cattle ranches and at Fort Huachuca, which was established during the Indian Wars of the 1870s and 1880s. It was the summer of 1877 when Tombstone founder Edward "Ed" Schieffelin first discovered silver in the hills of southern Arizona. He had been warned about prospecting so close to Apache warrior Cochise's stronghold. He recalled their words: "You'll find your tombstone if you don't stop running through this country all alone as you are while the Indians are so bad." But he was determined to see his discovery through. By August he was hot, out of provisions, and in need of clothes, so he headed to Tucson seeking investors. Sadly, no one took him seriously; he went back to the hills and recalled, "So I had to go back, as I came, only a little mad and more determined."

Ed eventually found an assayer named Richard Gird. Gird was an educated man from New York and ended up in Arizona, where he was engaged in assaying, superintending the construction of mills and furnaces, and surveying. Gird assessed the value of the ore when Ed met up with his brother Al, who was working with Gird. Ed's persistence finally paid off, and Richard told Ed that his easy-to-work ore was worth $40 to $2,000 per ton. On February 26, 1878, the three men arrived at the Brunckow house and built a shanty near the site. A month later they discovered the Lucky Cuss Mine. A little over a year later, on March 5, 1879, Tombstone proper was established on a 320-acre townsite and streets were laid out. The streets running east–west were named for citizens of territorial or local fame; the ones running north–south were simply numbered. Despite its lack of available freshwater, the camp grew rapidly, and water was delivered by carts from nearby Watervale.

Most businesses began in tents because building supplies and lumber were very scarce in the high desert and mining was a risky, unstable business. Tents were easily transported to the next boomtown if Tombstone's mines did not prove fruitful. Even Tombstone's first hotel began in a tent when Charles "Charley" Brown opened his Mohave Hotel. It eventually became a real building and was renamed Brown's Hotel on April 14, 1879, at the corner of 4th and Allen. In the beginning, the hotel averaged about twenty guests daily, but because people continuously flowed into Tombstone, Brown expanded his hotel. He also established the first restaurant in this location and soon had competition when Sam Sing opened a Chinese restaurant a couple months later.

Despite Tombstone's rapid growth, it was still a frontier mining camp in 1879. Approximately 900 people lived and worked in Tombstone, and the stages arrived daily with hopeful pioneers. It was clear that Tombstone would only grow more prosperous as the new year approached, because the existing mines were being worked diligently and new claims being staked daily. In 1880 Tombstone's mining camp took on a more civilized look as brick, frame, and adobe structures rapidly replaced the canvas tents, and the majority of townspeople were miners, assayers, freighters, and businessmen.

Devastating fires temporarily halted Tombstone's growth in 1881 and 1882. The June 22, 1881, blaze swept through half the town's newly developed business district and destroyed four blocks of businesses east of 5th Street. It was also in 1881 that the most well-known gun battle took place near the O.K. Corral. The feud between the Earp brothers and the band of bad guys known as the "Cowboys" came to a head on October 26, 1881. Once the smoke cleared from both events, Tombstone settled back into its noisy routine of mining, eating, and drinking.

The fire fiend struck again on May 25, 1882, destroying four blocks in the business district. This time the damage was west of 5th Street, the side the 1881 fire had spared. The flames spread quickly, and the fire showed no mercy. The fire quickly demolished most of Tombstone's largest hotels and restaurants, including Brown's, Bayley's

Restaurant, the Cosmopolitan Hotel, the Maison Doree, and the Grand Hotel. Tombstone recovered from its tragedies and rebuilt again, and the mills produced about $537,323 per month in 1882. As a result, Tombstone real estate became a valuable commodity. In 1882 Tombstone's real estate value was $917,491.50, substantially up compared to the territory's total real estate value in 1870, assessed at $538,355.

When the new year of 1883 arrived, Tombstone was a thriving, well-established city that offered residents and visitors alike very comfortable living conditions and delectable food. Tombstone's 5,000 to 6,000 residents had a hospital, a library, and private and public schools. Many enjoyed the numerous entertainments that included theaters, a skating rink, saloons, gaming rooms, a racetrack, an inground adobe swimming pool, and a bowling alley. Tombstone continued to offer first-class accommodations and fine dining, where tables were supplied with everything the market afforded. The mines produced rich, quality ore, even though more water began to surface in them. The water may have presented a problem at first, but once water pumps were installed and ore was struck below water level, confidence was bolstered.

By 1884 Tombstone was considered the greatest mining "camp" in the territory. Its mines produced ore that amounted to about $500,000 per month, and Tombstone flourished. The public school alone employed five teachers and averaged about 250 students on any given school day. The banks in town remained stable, and the Cochise County Bank maintained capital of $150,000. Personal property values continued to grow and exceeded $1.5 million.

Although some mines had begun to shut down, residents ended 1885 optimistically. The mines continued to generate enough ore with the help of water pumps, so most businesses remained open. The era was not over, and the people of Tombstone were determined to make a living in the mining town they called home. Times were changing, and the large Chinese population got caught up in the anti-Chinese movement that spread across the nation. The Pacific Chop House placed an advertisement that read, "The Chinese must go!" and "On March 1st, the Chinese now employed in the Pacific Chop House must go. D. J. Carter will assume control of the culinary department and W. L. Fenton will have charge of the dining room." Three years later, Carter was a janitor.

Residents and investors alike were optimistic when 1886 began, but all that changed on May 27. A disastrous fire completely leveled the Grand Central Mining

Works, and the mines flooded. Very little mining continued, and people started closing their businesses. Although a few had already left, the emigration was on a much larger scale now. Some remained, hoping the mines would again produce on the scale they once had. Unfortunately, large-scale mining never returned to Tombstone, and its population continued to decrease. The fact that many people were selling their property and leaving Tombstone showed the uncertainty they felt about the town's future. Without the mines, Tombstone's prosperity was in jeopardy. It's ironic to think that water, something so precious in Tombstone, eventually ended an era of high living the town would never again achieve.

Residents began physically removing their homes from the city so rapidly that the mayor and common council passed Ordinance 60 in April 1887, which prohibited houses and other buildings from being removed from town. The remaining houses were losing value, and Tombstone's property values dropped more than 50 percent from just four years earlier. Rumors spread as fast as the flames of Tombstone's disastrous fires. One was that the Girard Mill would join the other mines and shut down on May 1. The mill's superintendent attempted to quell that fear by stating that "the mill will run just so long as it can get water supply, and at present I know of no probability of such a thing happening as a failure in water. Of course, it is among the possibilities." Water eventually became a problem for all of them.

During its heyday, Tombstone glittered with gaslit restaurants that were beautifully decorated and often compared to the finest in San Francisco. Tombstone's restaurants advertised "the most elegantly appointed restaurant in the city" and the "best cooking and polite attentive service." Many were decorated with shimmering crystal chandeliers, plush Brussels carpets, and shiny walnut tables that were adorned with imported china, sparkling cut glass, and stylish silver cutlery. Imagine Doc Holliday or Ike Clanton sitting down to a meal of salmon with hollandaise sauce, ribs of beef, chicken fricassee, baked oyster pie, gumbo, potatoes, green peas, tomatoes, or blackberry pie.

Even though the patrons of these establishments ate elaborate meals in beautiful settings, weather and nature often interfered with the experience. Extreme hot and cold temperatures, pesky flies, and unbearable dust swirling in from the streets added to the dining experience. Tombstone sprinkled the streets with excess water from the mines, but when water was in great demand, none could be spared for the streets, and meals were served with a side of grit.

The meals themselves reflected the trends of the 1880s and did not include today's popular Southwestern fare. This was, after all, the Victorian era, when classic French cuisine was trendy and the menus were often printed in French. In late 1881 Tombstone's Grand Hotel restaurant finally changed the menu to English, and the *Epitaph* newspaper reported, "They have taken a new and very sensible departure by publishing its bill of fare in English, instead of French."

Not *all* of Tombstone's restaurants served French food. Many restaurant owners hailed from Europe because Tombstone's mines attracted a large influx of immigrants. The owners and cooks were from various ethnic backgrounds, and their cooking often reflected their heritages. Tombstone's restaurants and chophouses also served English, German, Italian, Irish, Creole, and New England cuisine. Even back in the day, a restaurant's chef made all the difference, and it was common for a restaurant to brag that their new cook was from the Pacific coast, San Francisco, or New Orleans.

Despite being in a remote location, Tombstone's cooks had no problem obtaining fresh meat for their meals. Wild game, beef, pork, chicken, lamb, and other meats were available at the local butcher shops. The Maison Doree restaurant in the Cosmopolitan Hotel offered "Chicken for breakfast and dinner, only $1, including wine; without wine the same as usual. . . . Wild game bought at the Maison Dore." Even though obtaining meat was easy, preparing the meals was not. Credit should be given to the people who prepared those meals, because their kitchens did not have today's modern conveniences such as food processors, blenders, bread machines, or mixers. Items we don't even think about, like mayonnaise, ketchup, sauces, and stocks, had to be made from scratch. Consider all the preparation time and effort that went into creating a meal when you look over the bills of fare (menus) and recipes.

A typical miner's wages were $3 per day, so many of them chose to eat at friends' houses, over an open fire, or in their tents rather than in the more glittering dining rooms. But it appears that the people of Tombstone ate well, whether in a restaurant dining room or behind bars in a jail cell. In addition to preparing meals for the patrons who dined at their establishments, several restaurateurs provided meals for prisoners staying in Tombstone's jail.

Throughout this book I've included tidbits of Tombstone's history, along with that of its restaurants, hotels, bakeries, meat markets, and mercantile stores. The recipes reflect actual dishes that were on the bills of fare advertised in their newspapers. They also include dishes prepared by home cooks and miners, and the ingredients are based on what was available to Tombstone's cooks at the time. I studied historic newspapers and old cookbooks—including some that were handed down through my family—to ensure that the recipes are truly typical of the late 1800s. I also used an 1875 cookbook that I purchased in Tombstone called *Breakfast, Luncheon and Tea* by Marion Harland as a source for these recipes. People came to Tombstone from all over and carried cookbooks with them from the East and Europe. There were also several cookbooks published in California at the time, so I've used them as well. One in particular, *The Physiology of Taste: Harder's Book of Practical American Cookery* by Jules Harder, comes from the chef de cuisine of the Palace Hotel, San Francisco, California. Many of Tombstone's residents hailed from England and Ireland and used *Mrs. Beeton's Dictionary of Every-day Cookery* by Isabella Beeton. Most Arizona papers of the time did not publish recipes, but California's frequently did. The San Francisco papers, which many Tombstone residents received, published scores of recipes that would have been used in Arizona. My two most treasured sources are from Tombstone connections. The first is Tombstone baker Otto Geisenhofer, whose daughter shared some of his recipes with me (back in the '90s). The other source is Isabelle "Belle" and Lena LeVan of the LeVan House, whose great-granddaughter, Robin Andrews, created a book of their recipes just for me. The LeVan House offered rooms and meals to people visiting Tombstone as well as to locals.

While these recipes are old-fashioned, you don't have to use old-fashioned methods to prepare them. A cake or pie recipe from the nineteenth century can be quite different from one created today. All the recipes in this book have been tested, and some slightly modified, to make them easier to re-create. The cooks of the 1880s would understand, and probably even be a little envious.

Tombstone's nineteenth-century restaurants, recipes, and meals were as sophisticated as the town itself. Despite being in a remote desert location, residents and visitors alike ate well. I think the only thing better than reading about its history is being able to taste it! Forks up!

Chapter One
IN THE BEGINNING: BREAKFAST AND BREAD

Most people in Tombstone ate breakfast at home, but those in hotels and boardinghouses enjoyed the hospitality of being fed. Bakeries often sold a variety of breads, but home cooks made delicious loaves for their families too. Hearty items like eggs, pancakes, steak, and other foods allowed people to work hard until the noonday meal.

SOURDOUGH BREAD ✒

While Ed Schieffelin and Richard Gird worked various mining sites in the Tombstone area in 1878, Ed's brother Al stayed at camp and cooked. Richard wrote this about Al's cooking: "Al was left in camp for obvious reasons—besides he was a boss cook, famous for his bread." It's not known what type of bread he made, but many miners carried sourdough starters with them. This basic sourdough begins with a starter, which can be found on the following page. This recipe was adapted from the *Sacramento Daily-Record Union*, May 12, 1883.

MAKES 1 LOAF

---

1 cup sourdough starter

½ cup milk, lukewarm

1 teaspoon salt

1 tablespoon sugar

2½–3 cups bread flour

Place starter in a large bowl; add the milk and stir. Next, add the salt and sugar and stir again. Add the flour and mix until well combined. Knead the dough on a lightly floured surface for about 10 minutes. Put the dough in a lightly oiled bowl and cover. Let the dough rise in a warm place (75°F–80°F) until doubled, about an hour. Punch down and let rise a second time. Punch down again, shape the dough, and place in a greased loaf pan or shape into loaves. Cover the dough and allow it to rise until doubled. Bake at 400°F for 40–45 minutes. Remove bread from the pan, and cool on a cake rack.

SOURDOUGH STARTER ❧

Sourdough starters were coveted and necessary, since yeast expired and supplies were often hard to obtain. Starters were traded, shared, and passed down through families. Many included potatoes, potato water, hops, salt, sugar, water, and flour to create perpetual or wild yeast. All they had to do was save a little from the original "starter" and refresh it with each use. They didn't call it sourdough; it was simply yeast to them.

While sourdough today is associated with California, it's not their invention—it's been around since Egyptian times. Emigrants and forty-niners made sourdough famous in California, but a French immigrant named Isidore Boudin took it to a whole new level. He opened a bakery in San Francisco in 1849 and made traditional French bread with local, wild yeast. The word "sourdough" wasn't used to describe bread until around the turn of the twentieth century. Bread was just bread, with different types of yeast. If an old recipe called for a cup of yeast, it was likely sourdough. If it called for a yeast cake, then it was regular yeast bread. The term also referred to people who were from Alaska or the Pacific Northwest. Back in the day it was a two-word description and later became a one-word descriptor. This recipe was adapted from the 1872 *California Recipe Book*.

2 cups potato water

2 cups flour

1 tablespoon sugar

¼ cup water

Note: Potato water can be made by boiling 4 potatoes in 3 cups water until the potatoes are soft.

Combine all ingredients in a glass bowl. Cover and allow to stand in a warm place for 48–72 hours to ferment. Once the mixture has begun to ferment and smells sour, it's ready. It should look like pancake batter. It should be stored loosely covered in the refrigerator (not too cold—around 45°F) until ready to use.

When you're ready to use the starter, remove the amount you need and allow it to come to room temperature. Once you remove some of the starter, you will need to replenish it. For example, if you remove 1 cup of starter, add 1 cup of flour and 1 cup of water. Stir to combine, and store in the refrigerator.

HOT ROLLS ✖

Delicious bakery items were the specialty of 22-year-old Bavarian baker Otto William Geisenhofer. He arrived with his older brother Michael, and they pitched a tent and set up Tombstone's first bakery at 529 Allen Street. The City Bakery opened in October 1879 and offered a variety of fresh baked goods including rolls, rye bread, pies, cakes, cookies, and candies. They not only sold baked goods to the general public; Otto also supplied Tombstone's hotels and mining camps just outside of town. According to Otto's daughter, Bertha Geisenhofer, when he first visited the United States, Otto said, "America is going to be the country of the future," which is why he decided to make it his new home. This recipe was adapted from Otto Geisenhofer's original recipe, written in German, which was shared by his daughter.

A photo of Otto when he lived in Tombstone
AUTHOR'S COLLECTION

MAKES 12 ROLLS

---

1 tablespoon dry yeast

1½ cups water (110°F)

2 teaspoons salt

4½–5 cups bread flour

Cornmeal

2 tablespoons butter, melted

In a large bowl, dissolve the yeast in ½ cup of the warm water. If using instant or rapid yeast, skip this step.

In a separate bowl, combine the salt and the remaining warm water. Pour this into the yeast mixture. Add 4 cups of the flour and mix well. If the dough seems sticky, gradually add flour as needed. Turn out onto a floured surface and knead for 10 minutes, or until dough is springy and smooth.

Place the dough in a lightly oiled bowl, cover, and allow to rise in a warm place (75°F–80°F) until doubled, about 2 hours. Punch the dough down and allow it to rise for another hour. Punch down again and tear off pieces the size of a medium onion. Cup your hands and roll the dough pieces into balls.

Place dough balls 2 inches apart on a cookie sheet that has been sprinkled with cornmeal, continuing until all the dough has been used. Using the palm of your hand, flatten each roll. Cover and allow to rise until doubled, about 45 minutes. Brush the rolls with the melted butter and bake at 425°F for 15 minutes.

WHITE BREAD ✖

Another Bavarian baker, Joseph Stumpf, arrived in town around the same time as Otto. He arrived with his wife, Flora, and their three children to open the American Bakery on March 15, 1879. Stumpf's bakery was located at 215 5th Street, where he supplied Tombstone's families with breads, pies, and assorted cakes. This recipe was adapted from Marion Harland's *Breakfast, Luncheon and Tea*, 1875.

MAKES 1 LOAF

¼ cup buttermilk

¼ cup butter, melted

2 eggs, lightly beaten

¼ cup water

2 tablespoons sugar

1 package rapid or instant yeast

1 teaspoon salt

3–3½ cups bread flour

2 teaspoons butter, melted

In a large bowl, combine the buttermilk, butter, eggs, water, and sugar.

Combine the yeast, salt, and 3 cups of the flour and add to the buttermilk mixture. Mix well and add enough flour to form a soft but not sticky dough.

Knead on a floured surface for about 10 minutes. You will know that you have kneaded enough when you press a finger in the dough and it bounces back.

Place the dough in a lightly oiled bowl, turn to coat the surface, and cover with a towel or plastic wrap. Allow the dough to double in size in a warm place, about 1 hour.

Remove the dough from the bowl and roll into a rectangular shape on a floured surface. Starting at the shortest end, roll the dough up like a jelly roll. Tuck the ends under and place in a greased 9-inch loaf pan. Allow this to rise under a towel in a warm place until doubled.

Once the dough has risen again, brush the top with the melted butter and bake at 375°F for 30 minutes.

Remove the bread from the pan and cool on a cake rack.

BAKING POWDER BISCUITS ❧

Tombstone merchants like P. W. Smith and James McKean and Isaac Knight kept a full line of groceries and provisions so that Tombstone cooks could make tasty meals. Many made a special point of supplying fruits, butter, flour, baking powder and soda, grains, eggs, cheese, and potatoes from California. This recipe was adapted from the *Tombstone Daily Epitaph*, November 9, 1889.

SERVES 6–8

2½ cups flour

½ teaspoon baking soda

½ teaspoon salt

1 tablespoon lard or butter

1 cup buttermilk

Note: For an extra-special treat, try adding ½ cup shredded cheese and ½ teaspoon of your favorite herb to the batter before rolling.

Combine the flour, soda, and salt in a large bowl.

Cut in the lard or butter to form pea-size pieces.

Add the buttermilk and stir just to combine. Do not overbeat.

Gently knead dough one or two times on a heavily floured surface.

Roll out to ½-inch thickness. Cut into rounds with a biscuit cutter or empty tin can. Place in a greased skillet or baking pan.

Bake at 450°F for 10–15 minutes or until golden.

MISSISSIPPI CORNBREAD ✐

It may seem out of place in Tombstone, but cooks from all over came to make it rich, whether in the mines or in a kitchen. Some of them were Mississippi riverboat cooks, which is why this recipe would have been quite normal in some restaurants. This recipe was adapted from Marion Harland's *Breakfast, Luncheon and Tea*, 1875.

MAKES 1 LOAF

1 cup cornmeal

1 cup bread flour

½ teaspoon baking soda

½ teaspoon salt

¼ cup sugar

2 tablespoons butter, melted

1¼ cups milk

2 eggs, beaten

Combine all the dry ingredients in a large bowl. Add the milk and eggs and blend until the batter is lump free. Pour into a greased loaf pan or 8-inch cake tin, and bake for 30–40 minutes at 350°F. Serve warm or cold.

BUTTERMILK HOT CAKES ❧

Hot cakes, or pancakes, were a quick and hearty meal that required only a handful of ingredients that were readily available from local merchants like Cadwell and Stanford. These two young men, aged twenty-six and twenty-one, respectively, moved from nearby Watervale and built a brick store on Fremont Street, where they stocked a full line of staple goods for people arriving to stake their claims and begin life in Tombstone. This recipe was adapted from the 1872 *California Recipe Book*.

SERVES 4

2½ cups flour

½ teaspoon salt

1 teaspoon baking soda

1½ cups buttermilk

1 teaspoon melted butter

Water

Note: If you do not have buttermilk, add 1 teaspoon vinegar to 1 cup milk. Let stand for 5 minutes, then stir and use.

Sift dry ingredients into a large bowl. Add the buttermilk and butter, and combine with the dry ingredients. If the batter is too thick, add water to get a good consistency, which depends on your thickness preference. Using a ladle or spoon, pour batter onto a hot greased griddle or frying pan. Cook over medium-high heat until bubbles appear on the batter. Turn and cook for about 1 minute longer. Serve warm with butter and maple syrup. Garnish with orange slices or wedges.

A COWBOY RESTAURATEUR

Joseph Isaac "Ike" Clanton, an anti-Earp participant in the infamous gunfight at the O.K. Corral, was first and foremost a businessman. His Star Restaurant, one of the first to serve meals to Tombstone's pioneers, was located in the area known as the Mill Site. The *Arizona Weekly Star* reported on December 12, 1878: "Tombstone Mill Site is now the scene of activity. Houses, shanties, and jacals are going up rapidly, and several families are on the ground. A restaurant has been opened by Mr. Isaac 'Ike' Clanton." Clanton placed an order with Lionel M. Jacobs in Tucson on December 22, 1878. He sent $150 cash with his courier, J. E. Bailey, to buy $350 worth of groceries and the balance to be put on his account. His letter instructed, "I will pay only in greenbacks and wish you to sell to me at greenback price. . . . Yours very respectfully, Isaac Clanton." Some of the items he ordered included dried apples and peaches, lard, coffee, canned tomatoes, raisins, salt, pepper, syrup, flour, dishes, glasses, towels, cream of tartar, sugar, and cornmeal. His order has survived for more than a century, offering a glimpse into the history of the region.

Ike Clanton wrote this letter in December 1878 when he ordered supplies to start his Star Restaurant.
UNIVERSITY OF ARIZONA, SPECIAL COLLECTIONS, JACOBS FILE.

GERMAN PANCAKES ✌

Often called "Dutch Baby" during the 1880s, the recipes for this puffy pancake vary slightly, but this is a classic version from New Orleans, Louisiana's, the *Daily Picayune*, October 8, 1882. The ingredients are about the same from recipe to recipe, but some early versions directed to bake in an oven, while others recommended cooking over a fire in a cast iron pan.

SERVES 4–8

4 eggs, separated

1 cup flour

¼ teaspoon salt

1 cup milk

3 tablespoons butter, melted

Place the egg yolks and egg whites in separate bowls. Beat the yolks for about 3 minutes, until light in color. Next beat the egg whites until stiff. Combine the yolks and whites together and add the remaining ingredients except the butter. Gently fold or stir to blend.

Use a 9 × 13-inch pan, cake pans, or about six large muffin tins. Place the butter in the pan and then add the batter.

Bake at 400°F for about 20 minutes, or until puffy and golden.

Serve with jam or powdered sugar.

BUCKWHEAT CAKES

Whenever I think of these pancakes, I remember my childhood days when my family visited my parents' hometown in upstate New York. This recipe is from my grandmother, Anna Louise White-Teeter, from the early 1900s. She taught her daughters how to make them, and my Aunt Myrtle shared the recipe with me. Her recipe calls for a thinner batter, but modify as you like. Recipes like these were lovingly carted across the frontier by eastern pioneers and appeared on Tombstone's menus.

MAKES 12–15

1½ cups buckwheat flour

1 cup white flour

1 teaspoon salt

1½ cups buttermilk

½ cup hot water

¼ cup boiling water

1 teaspoon baking soda

Note: If you don't have buttermilk, you can make a substitute by adding 1 teaspoon vinegar to 1 cup milk. Let stand for 5 minutes; stir and use.

In a large bowl, combine the flours and salt. Add the buttermilk and ½ cup hot water. Mix well and cover. Allow this mixture to sit overnight in a warm place.

The next morning, combine the ¼ cup boiling water and the baking soda in a small bowl. When the mixture bubbles, add it to the buckwheat mixture and stir to blend.

Cook on a hot griddle or frying pan, just as you would pancakes. Serve immediately with butter and syrup.

CORN BATTER CAKES ✒

In July 1879 one of the most elegant hotels was opened by Carl Gustav "Gus" Bilicke and his son, Albert, even though it began as a tent structure at 407–411 Allen. The Bilickes offered the first real beds in Tombstone, and guests enjoyed music being played on a Steinway piano. All the hotels offered meals to their guests, which included breakfast. This recipe was adapted from Marion Harland's *Breakfast, Luncheon and Tea*, 1875.

SERVES 4

½ cup cornmeal

1½ cups water

2¼ cups flour

⅓ cup sugar

1¼ teaspoons baking powder

1 teaspoon salt

1 cup milk

1 egg, beaten

2 tablespoons butter, melted

Orange slices

In a medium saucepan, bring the water to a boil; add the cornmeal and boil for 5 minutes.

In a large bowl, combine the dry ingredients. Mix well. Add the cornmeal mixture, milk, egg, and butter. Stir to combine, being sure not to overmix the batter.

Cook on a griddle or in a frying pan, as you would pancakes. Serve warm, with butter and jelly or your favorite syrup. Garnish with orange slices.

OMELET ✺

Local chickens produced eggs in Tombstone, so there was no shortage for cooking. Omelets were often served as a main meal, at tea times, or for lunch. The Cosmopolitan Hotel's dining room served ham and eggs every day for breakfast. This is a basic omelet recipe that's been adapted from the 1872 *California Recipe Book*, but it can be used for the basis of many delicious recipes. Try filling the omelet with cheese, ham, bacon, peppers, onions, mushrooms, or anything else you'd like to experiment with.

SERVES 1

3 eggs

¼ teaspoon salt

⅛ teaspoon freshly ground pepper

1 teaspoon water

1 tablespoon butter

Beat the eggs, salt, pepper, and water in a medium bowl until the eggs are frothy.

Melt the butter in an omelet pan or nonstick skillet over medium-high heat. Once the butter begins to bubble, add the eggs. Let the eggs cook untouched for 1 minute. Using a spatula, gently draw the edges of the omelet to the center while tipping the pan at an angle. This will allow the uncooked center to run to the outside; do this in several places.

Cover the pan and allow the omelet to cook for 2 to 3 minutes, or until the center is firm. Fold in half and serve.

This photo, taken shortly after the 1881 fire, shows how the verandas were torn off to stop the fire from spreading. Circa 1882
COURTESY OF THE CALIFORNIA HISTORY ROOM, CALIFORNIA STATE LIBRARY, SACRAMENTO, CALIFORNIA

PORK SAUSAGE ℀

People living in Tombstone relied on butchers like 35-year-old German immigrant Apollinar Bauer. He was one of Tombstone's pioneer butchers and in December 1879 opened the U.S. Market at 318 Fremont Street. In addition to his butchering skills, Bauer was known to pluck melodious sounds from his German zither. He was quite proficient at playing the instrument and gave lessons to some of the other townspeople, who referred to him as "Zither Bauer." He sold not only a variety of meats but also sausages. This recipe was adapted from the *San Francisco Bulletin*, December 7, 1878.

MAKES 1 POUND

1 pound ground pork (or pork butt that you grind)

1 tablespoon dried sage

2 teaspoons dried savory or marjoram

1 teaspoon salt

¼ teaspoon freshly ground pepper

Mix all the ingredients together. It can be tested for seasoning, but it must be cooked. Cook a small amount of mixture, taste for seasoning, and add as you like. When ready, shape into patties and fry over medium heat until no longer pink inside.

Note: Feel free to add your own seasonings, such as pepper flakes, garlic powder, onion, etc.

BEEF SAUSAGE ❧

Another butcher shop was the Cosmopolitan Market, opened by the Tribolet brothers of Switzerland. Their adobe store on 5th Street carried all varieties of meats and specialized in domestic and imported sausages. The five brothers, Abraham, Charles, Godfrey, Robert, and Siegfried, though originally involved in the butchering business, eventually become general contractors, restaurateurs, landowners, brewers, and saloonkeepers. The Cosmopolitan, later called the Eagle Market, was managed by Godfrey, one of the middle brothers, who later became a city councilor. This recipe was adapted from *Mrs. Beeton's Dictionary of Every-day Cookery*.

MAKES 3 POUNDS

3 pounds beef chuck roast or 80–85 percent lean ground beef

5 garlic cloves, diced

1 tablespoon sage

¾ tablespoon salt

¾ tablespoon black pepper

⅛ teaspoon red pepper flakes

½ teaspoon dry mustard

If using chuck, cut into 1-inch pieces, set in the freezer for 2 hours, and then grind. Once ground, add the seasonings and shape into patties. Fry in a large skillet over medium heat until no longer pink.

HOT CHOCOLATE ✦

Today we call this beverage "hot chocolate," but back in the day it was just referred to as chocolate. Everyone knew that it meant a hot beverage that was served at tea time alongside coffee and tea. It was also a treat, because chocolate was a luxury. Cocoa powder was more readily available. This recipe was adapted from *Cocoa and Chocolate: A Short History of Their Production and Use, 1886.*

SERVES 2

½ square dark chocolate or 1 heaping tablespoon chocolate chips

1 tablespoon sugar (if using unsweetened chocolate)

1 tablespoon hot water

1 cup milk

Whipped cream

Place the chocolate, sugar, and water into a saucepan. Allow chocolate to melt slowly over low heat. Use a whisk to blend until smooth and glossy.

Add the milk and allow to warm, but do not boil. Serve in teacups and garnish with fresh whipped cream.

Chapter Two

GETTING STARTED: SOUPS, STEWS, AND SALADS

These items would all fall under the appetizer category by today's standards, but during the nineteenth century, they were all separate. People ate their way through courses and began with soup or stew. Salads were mayonnaise based and often served as a meal or a side and included lobster, shrimp, and chicken.

OYSTER SOUP ✑

Oysters were the nineteenth century's trendiest food, and Tombstone served plenty of them. Some canned and some fresh, when in season (when the months of the year have an "R" in them). Twenty-five-year-old Englishman William Shilliam had a general merchandise store on 4th between Allen and Fremont Streets where he carried groceries and provisions, as well as fresh, aka "green," California fruit. His customers included hotels, restaurants, dealers, and camps near the mines. Shilliam, along with most other merchants, advertised fresh fish for sale, and oysters were his specialty. This recipe was adapted from San Francisco's *Daily Examiner*, December 23, 1883.

SERVES 6

4 cups oysters

¾ cup water

⅓ cup butter or margarine

⅓ cup flour

2 cups milk

2 cups cream

1 slice of onion

1 small bay leaf

1 stalk celery

Salt and pepper to taste

1 teaspoon mace or nutmeg

1 parsley sprig to garnish

Clean and shuck oysters, and chop them coarsely. Place the oysters in a large pot, add the water, and bring to a boil over medium heat. Remove the pot from heat and drain, reserving the oyster liquor. Set oysters aside in a bowl.

In the same pot, melt the butter and add the flour, stirring to make a roux. Add the reserved liquor and blend until smooth. Set aside on the stove to keep warm.

In a separate pot, scald the milk and remaining ingredients. Strain the milk into the thickened roux and mix until combined. Add the oysters to the pot and stir. Serve immediately, garnished with a fresh parsley sprig.

RURAL HOUSE

This establishment was opened in January 1880 by Tucson civil engineer and architect Henry G. Howe at 521 Allen Street. He hired New Yorkers John and Lavina Campbell Holly to manage it. While both Hollys managed the Rural House, it was Lavina's name that would be associated with it. The *Arizona Daily Star* wrote in November 1879: "Mrs. L.C. Holly will take charge of the culinary department, which ensures a good table, with all the delicacies." Her success may have been attributed to her father, who was a hotel man in Franklin, Pennsylvania. Not long after taking charge of the house, John broke a couple ribs and took laudanum, a common drug of the time, to alleviate the pain. Sadly, he died from an overdose on January 23. The 32-year-old Lavina had no choice but to continue on with the business so she could support her two young daughters. She continued to work in the restaurant business for several years, but expanded her interests when she purchased and worked several Arizona mines.

Lavina left the Rural House to operate the Grand Hotel, and George Rutledge and James Crowley purchased the Rural House from her in June 1880. Shortly thereafter, on July 12, Rutledge and Crowley dissolved their partnership, but James remained the proprietor of the house. He hired Mrs. Carrie Hanson, a 32-year-old native of Denmark, to manage the dining room. Hanson was no newcomer to this field; in fact, she was quite experienced. When she first came to Tombstone, she worked for Semantha Fallon at the San Jose House and then became proprietor of the Miner's Boarding House, located at the corner of 5th and Toughnut. Hanson left Tombstone a couple of years later to open her own restaurant in Johnson, Arizona. The Rural House was no more, but in October, Edward Rafferty opened the Miner's Restaurant at the Rural House's former location. His restaurant not only served food but also doubled as a retail and wholesale liquor business.

TOMATO SOUP ✑

Tucson's *Arizona Daily Star* frequently printed articles from Tombstone residents like Wells Spicer, who sent reports to them on the progress and activities in the town. Wells later became an important judge in Tombstone. In February 1880 he reported that the various stages coming to town were well loaded, especially with women and children. He also reported that Tombstone had more restaurants, saloons, gambling houses, and dance houses than any other village, town, or city in Arizona. He wrote, "It is the boss town." Soups began almost every meal in Tombstone's restaurants, and tomato was easy to make and have on hand. This recipe was adapted from the *Arizona Daily Star*, July 4, 1882.

SERVES 4

2 tablespoons butter

1 carrot, peeled and sliced

1 turnip, peeled and sliced

1 onion, peeled and sliced

1 stalk celery, sliced

4 tablespoons flour

4 cups beef or vegetable broth

1 (28-ounce) can or 3 cups chopped fresh tomatoes

1 bay leaf

1 pinch of freshly grated nutmeg

½ teaspoon salt

⅛ teaspoon freshly ground pepper

Croutons to garnish

Melt the butter in a large pot. Cook the carrot, turnip, onion, and celery in the butter over medium-high heat. Once the mixture is golden, add the flour. Cook for an additional 2 minutes. Add the remaining ingredients and bring to a boil. Reduce the heat to low and cook until all the vegetables are tender.

Remove from heat and force the mixture through a sieve, or puree and strain. Season to taste with salt and pepper.

Return the pot to the stove and bring soup to a boil. Top with warm croutons and/or foamed butter. (To make foamed butter, melt some butter and then beat it with a whisk until foamy.)

Note: To reduce the acidity in this recipe, dissolve 1 teaspoon baking soda in 2 tablespoons water. Pour mixture into soup after you have reduced the heat.

TOMBSTONE'S GROCERS

The *Arizona Daily Star* reported that P. W. Smith's general store had received a train car full of merchandise in 1880 that would have included clothing, dry goods, liquors, hardware, and groceries. Smith and other merchants bought a large portion of their goods directly from California companies, but they also purchased items from mercantile and warehouse firms in Tucson. L. Zeckendorf had one of the largest firms in Tucson. In fact, he did so much business with Tombstone merchants that he eventually opened a branch office there.

The grocery stores of the 1800s hardly resembled the ones today. They more closely resembled mercantile stores where food, textiles, and provisions for miners and prospectors were sold. By June 1880 Tombstone had approximately sixteen mercantile stores. Because the majority of their customers were associated with mining, many of the grocery and mercantile stores allowed patrons to purchase on credit, which was needed when wages were paid sporadically. Some merchants kept running tabs for credit-paying customers; others required that customers maintain credit books. The patrons brought their books with them to make purchases on credit. Because this was risky for the merchants, they charged higher rates for credit purchases. Those who could pay cash were offered a discount.

California Store, Tombstone, Arizona.

This store sold stationery, provisions, liquors, tobacco, cigars, dry goods, ranch butter, fresh salmon and mackerel, and a variety of other groceries. Circa 1880
COURTESY OF THE CALIFORNIA HISTORY ROOM, CALIFORNIA STATE LIBRARY, SACRAMENTO, CALIFORNIA

CONSOMMÉ WITH MUSHROOMS 🙠 (CONSOMMÉ AUX CHAMPIGNONS)

Tasker and Pridham's mercantile was at the corner of 5th and Allen Streets and owned by Joseph Tasker and George Pridham. They quickly became one of the leading general merchants and carried a variety of goods that included groceries, produce, liquor, and California and imported wines. They catered to their large mining clientele by offering a full line of items needed to outfit miners. The Boss Store, P. W. Smith's, and Nellie Cashman's Nevada Cash Store also advertised: "Fresh fruits received daily from Los Angeles." Michael Edwards's California Variety Store offered an array of items for chefs and home cooks. Many merchants sold fresh and dried products like apples and mushrooms that were turned into delicious meals in Tombstone, like this recipe, adapted from *Mrs. Beeton's Dictionary of Every-day Cookery.*

SERVES 4-6

½ pound mushrooms, sliced

4 cups beef stock or consommé

Chives to garnish

Boil the mushrooms and 1 cup of the stock in a large sauté pan over medium heat for about 10 minutes. Divide the remaining stock and mushroom broth into serving bowls. Garnish with chives.

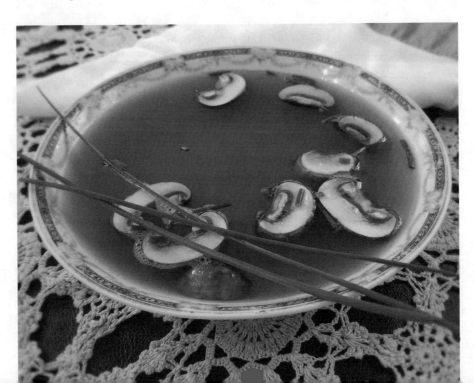

CHICKEN SOUP ✺

Apollinar Bauer of the U.S. Market partnered with Arizona Territory cattle baron Henry Clay Hooker, who owned the well-known Sierra Bonita Ranch in early 1880. It was at this ranch that Wyatt and Warren Earp and others rested while pursuing the men who had robbed the Kinnear stagecoach. Apollinar Bauer and Henry Hooker's new business was called Hooker and Bauer's, and their shop was situated at Apollinar's original business location of 4th and Fremont Streets. In August, Bauer sold half his lots to Hooker for $300; they promised to supply the best beef from American-fed cattle and vowed to "defy competition." Butchers like Bauer sold not only beef but also a variety of other meats, including pork, mutton, wild game, and chicken. Chicken soup was a way to make a meal for a large crowd and serve quickly at restaurants. This recipe was adapted from *One Thousand and One Useful Recipes and Valuable Hints About Cooking and Housekeeping.*

SERVES 6

3- to 4-pound chicken, quartered

2–3 quarts water

2 stalks celery

1 onion, chopped

½ cup diced celery

1 tablespoon chopped parsley

1 cup sliced carrots

½ teaspoon salt

¼ teaspoon freshly ground pepper

1–2 cups cooked egg noodles

Boil water, chicken, celery stalks, and onion in a large stockpot for about 45 minutes, or until the chicken is tender. Skim the top of the stock to remove foam if needed. Remove and debone the chicken.

Strain and measure 4 cups of the stock, and add the remaining ingredients except the egg noodles; simmer, covered, for 20 minutes or until carrots are tender. Add egg noodles and serve.

THE BEEF TRADE

Most of Tombstone's butchers purchased their cattle by the hundreds and had their own corrals and slaughterhouses. By 1880 there were four in town. A little over a year later, that number had doubled. Many of them advertised that their cattle were "American," meaning, supposedly, that the cattle were not rustled illegally across the Mexican border, as many were at the time. But not all butchers were honest in their business practices or advertising. Some cattle were considered so "hot" you barely needed to cook them! Beef was an important commodity in Tombstone and its nearby ranches, so people worried when news of a beef shortage was reported in late 1881. Ranchers said that unless large shipments were imported, beef cattle would be in short supply within three months of the announcement. Owners of some of the largest ranches moved their stock to other areas because of a recent Indian scare and the depredations of cattle thieves. Local business owners and residents made trips almost daily to the meat market simply because they couldn't stock up, as there was no place to store the meat. Tombstone had ice and iceboxes for storage, but the technology hardly compared to the refrigerators and freezers of today.

STEWED BEEF ❧

Irishman Thomas Patrick Ward opened the City Meat Market on Allen Street and also owned a ranch that included a house, a spring, and a variety of livestock. Luckily for Tombstone's residents, his corral and slaughterhouse were located outside of town on his ranch, along Babocomari Creek. His competitor, Apollinar Bauer, also established his own corral and slaughterhouse. Wholesalers and retailers alike called on them to make their meat purchases, but Bauer found a way to edge his competition by offering free deliveries to all parts of town. This recipe was adapted from California's *Sacramento Daily Record-Union*, April 30, 1881.

SERVES 4

---

5 tablespoons bacon fat or oil

3 pounds beef, cubed

2 large onions, sliced

1 tablespoon marjoram

3 tablespoons flour

2 teaspoons salt

½ teaspoon freshly ground pepper

3 cups beef stock

2 tablespoons ketchup

1 cup sliced carrots

Heat 3 tablespoons bacon fat in a large stockpot over high heat. Add the cubed beef and brown on all sides. Transfer the meat to a plate or bowl.

Sauté the onions and marjoram in the remaining 2 tablespoons bacon fat over medium heat. Cook for about 10 minutes, or until the onions have turned golden. Sprinkle with flour, salt, and pepper. Add the cooked beef back to the pot. Stir well to incorporate the flour, and cook for about 3 minutes. Add the stock, ketchup, and carrots and bring to a boil. Reduce the heat, cover, and simmer for 2–2½ hours, or until tender.

TOMBSTONE EXPANDS IN 1880

As the town grew and people continued to arrive in Tombstone with the hope of striking it rich, the concern over water was also growing. The water brought to town was largely consumed by the building trade, which created shortages for bathing and cooking. Tombstone eventually had its own water source, but not for a couple more dry and dusty months. Although the dust made life uncomfortable, it didn't prevent hopeful entrepreneurs from opening their businesses. Some fifteen restaurants and dining halls supported a population of about 2,000. Some of the newest restaurants in Tombstone were an Italian restaurant, the Golden Eagle, the Bodie, and the Star, run by Lucy Young and Belle Sullivan, and Delmonico's, a popular name for restaurants all over the West. Because Delmonico's was synonymous with elegant dining and fine cuisine, many Easterners who went west named their restaurants for the New York icon. While Delmonico's had a couple locations in New York City during the 1800s, they were not a chain. Of course the ones on the frontier weren't associated with them at all, but diners knew the name and had great expectations. More restaurants opened by the time the desert flowers began to bloom. There were also Lukini and Staglono's chophouse, Peter Marcovich's Queen Chop House, William Smith's restaurant, and Wong Fong's restaurant. Shortly thereafter, 28-year-old Frank Herbert Carleton opened Carleton's Coffee, Oyster, and Chop House at 523 Allen Street. Like many others, Frank served just about everyone, including miners, gamblers, and businessmen. Patrons also visited the Gem Coffee and Ice Cream Parlor on Allen if they desired hot chocolate, coffee, oysters, chops, or ice cream. In mid-1880 Mrs. Merrill opened the Boston House on 4th, but she became the proprietor of the Cosmopolitan Hotel Dining Room shortly after. In addition to trendy French food, they served fresh fish and shellfish, which was transported by train from California and the East Coast in refrigerated cars lined with ice chunks and hay. They got their supplies from merchants who advertised oysters shipped by express from Baltimore, Maryland. With Mrs. Merrill presiding over the dining room, the Cosmopolitan was well on its way to being established as one of Tombstone's best. A few months later, J. W. Cameron replaced her, but the restaurant continued to attract customers.

COSMOPOLITAN RESTAURANT.

J. W. CAMERON, PROPRIETOR.

BILL OF FARE.

DINNER.

SOUPS.
CHICKEN.

BOILED.
LEG OF MUTTOON, *Caper Sauce.*

ROAST.
SIRLOIN OF BEEF.   VENISON, CURRANT JELLY.
PORK WITH APPLE SAUCE.   MUTTON.

ENTREES.
CHICKEN FRICASSEE.   SCALLOPED ANTELOPE.
HAM, A LA REIGAN, *Champagne Sauce.*   OYSTER PATTIES.

VEGETABLES.
ASSORTED.

PASTRY.
ENGLISH PLUM PUDDING, *Queen Sauce.*
MINCE PIE.   CURRANT PIE.

DESSERT.
APPLES.   NUTS.   RAISINS.

TEA.   COFFEE.

An actual menu that customers perused at the restaurant
COURTESY MARGE ELLIOTT

OYSTER STEW ✦

Back in the day, oyster stew contained nothing but oysters, cream, and butter, with some seasoning. Oyster soup, on the other hand, contained aromatics like onions and other seasonings. The Cosmopolitan Hotel's dining room was said to be one of the finest in the Arizona Territory and offered trendy dishes of the time that included oysters. This recipe was adapted from the *Tombstone Epitaph*, January 18, 1890.

SERVES 4–6

1 quart oysters, fresh (shucked) or canned

¾ cup water

¼ cup butter

½ teaspoon salt

4 cups milk, scalded

Parsley to garnish

Place cleaned oysters in a large stockpot; add the water and slowly bring to a boil, until the oysters open. Strain, reserving the oyster liquor. Put the oysters, oyster liquor, butter, and salt back in the large stockpot. Simmer until the edges of the oysters begin to curl.

While waiting for the oysters to curl, scald the milk in a saucepan. Add the scalded milk to the oysters once they have curled. Garnish with parsley and serve immediately with French bread.

MULLIGATAWNY ✖

The Western expansion happened roughly along the same timeline as the Victorian era, 1860–1900, when Queen Victoria ruled England and its empire, which included India. This recipe shows the influence of the Indian culture during that time, and "mulligatawny" translates to "pepper water" in India. This soup incorporates many of the exotic spices used in Indian cuisine. This recipe was adapted from the *Tombstone Epitaph*, February 15, 1890.

SERVES 4–6

¼ cup butter

1 cup diced chicken

¼ cup chopped onion

¼ cup chopped celery

Sprig of parsley

¼ cup chopped carrot

1 green pepper, diced

¼ cup flour

1 teaspoon curry powder

2 cloves

½ teaspoon mace

½ teaspoon salt

⅛ teaspoon freshly ground pepper

1 apple, diced

1 cup diced tomatoes

4 cups chicken stock

Melt the butter in a large pot over medium heat. Cook the chicken and vegetables in the butter over medium-high heat until lightly brown. Add the flour and spices and stir well. Next, add the apple, tomatoes, and chicken stock; simmer for 40 minutes. Taste for seasoning, and adjust to taste with more salt and pepper. Serve with steamed rice.

CHICKEN GUMBO ✌

Joseph Pascholy was a 30-year-old Swiss immigrant who owned the Arcade Restaurant in 1880. He wanted his diners to feel like they had entered a first-class French café, so he added trendy wallpaper, paneled walls, and private dining rooms. He also owned the Occidental Saloon and restaurant at 429 Allen Street and hired Aristotle Petro to manage the restaurant. The business was known by two names; the *Epitaph* preferred "chop house," while the *Nugget* always used "restaurant." Regardless of what it was called, Petro offered extravagant French cuisine and hired Alvan Young. Young had cooked in some of the largest hotels and rotisseries on the Pacific coast and was also a cook on a Mississippi River steamboat. This recipe, adapted from *The Physiology of Taste: Harder's Book of Practical American Recipe Cookery*, 1885, shows his background.

SERVES 4–6

2- to 3-pound chicken

2 quarts water

2 cups thickly sliced okra

1 teaspoon cayenne pepper sauce

1 teaspoon thyme

½ teaspoon salt

1 tablespoon parsley

¼ teaspoon freshly ground pepper

¼ cup dry breadcrumbs

1 tablespoon Worcestershire sauce

1 tablespoon butter or margarine

Place the chicken and water in a large stockpot and bring to a boil. Cook until the chicken is completely cooked and tender, about 1 hour. Remove the chicken, debone, and set aside.

Skim excess fat from the chicken stock. Add the okra and cook over medium-high heat for 15 minutes. Add the chicken and remaining ingredients, and stir until heated through. Serve with crusty French bread.

CHICKEN SALAD ✣

As Tombstone continued to grow and improve, Charley Brown of Brown's Hotel tore down his one-story wood-frame hotel in June 1880 and began construction of a new two-story structure. He hired Tucson city architect and restaurateur H. G. Howe to design it. The new hotel was brick and accommodated about 100 to 150 guests. Since Brown's hotel was growing quickly, he needed a manager. As he browsed through the local want ads, he found George Bayley's request for a position as a manager in a hotel or restaurant. Brown hired Bayley to manage both Brown's Hotel and its restaurant, which became known as Bayley's Restaurant. Bayley was a good choice, because he brought twenty years of experience from the California hotel business. The restaurant was next to the hotel at 403 Allen Street and could feed 300 people at any given meal. This recipe was adapted from the 1872 *California Recipe Book*.

SERVES 2

2 cups cooked chicken

½ cup diced celery

¼ to ½ cup Homemade Mayonnaise (see recipe on page 116)

Lettuce leaves

Capers for garnish, optional

Boil a chicken and remove the meat. Cut or tear into bite-size pieces. Add the celery and mayonnaise and stir to combine. Place a scoop of the salad into a lettuce leaf, and garnish with a few capers.

Brown's Hotel is the building to the left of the restaurant. It doesn't look like much from this angle because the main entrance was on the other side, on Allen Street. Circa 1880.
COURTESY OF THE CALIFORNIA HISTORY ROOM, CALIFORNIA STATE LIBRARY, SACRAMENTO, CALIFORNIA

THE ICE MAN COMETH

The summer months of 1880 brought modern conveniences to Tombstone. The Western Union telegraph arrived, water pipes were laid by the Sycamore Springs Water Company, and Tombstone was receiving four large chunks of ice daily. The *Tombstone Daily Nugget* also reported that plans for an ice factory in nearby Charleston were being made and that five 1-ton-capacity ice machines had already been shipped. Even though there was ice in town, business owners and residents visited meat markets almost daily because they couldn't stock up. Tombstone had iceboxes for storage, but the technology hardly compared to the refrigerators and freezers of today. By 1885 F. C. Hawkins of the Natural Ice Company was selling ice at 3 cents per pound and offered free delivery. Hawkins had competition from Julius Caesar and Ben Wehrfritz, co-owners of the Crystal Palace Saloon. They offered ice at 2½ cents per pound and announced that they kept a large supply constantly on hand with no danger of selling out, but they did not mention free delivery. Hawkins left Tombstone that September for Denver, Colorado.

GRAND HOTEL

On September 9, 1880, Lavina Holly, formerly of the Rural House, opened Tombstone's third, and reportedly finest, hotel and restaurant. The Grand was a gem, centrally located at 424–426 Allen Street, and sat almost opposite the Cosmopolitan Hotel, now a two-story building with orange trees. It was just down the block from Brown's Hotel, too. An *Epitaph* reporter was given a preopening inspection of the Grand and its restaurant. The headline of his article, "Tombstone's New Hotel—The Most Elegant Hostelry in Arizona," sums up his observations. He wrote: "The first thing to strike the eye is the wide and handsome staircase, covered by an elegant carpet and supporting a heavy black walnut baluster . . . a heavy Brussels carpet of the most elegant style and finish graces the floor; the walls are adorned with rare and costly paintings; the furniture is of walnut, cushioned with the most expensive silk; and nothing lacks, save the piano, which will be in place shortly."

The Grand's dining room shimmered with three elegant chandeliers that hung from their center pieces and walnut tables covered with cut glass, china, silver salt and pepper shakers, and the latest style of cutlery. Messrs. Devern and Whitehead oversaw a kitchen that contained an elegant Montagin range with a broiler, sinks with hot and cold water, and "all the appliances necessary to feed five hundred persons at a few hours' notice." On September 15, miner and diarist George Parsons dined at the Grand Hotel and wrote, "It is the best place I've been thus far in the territory. Something like a hotel. Best meal yet and best served. Popular prices too—only four bits."

By April 1881, Jessie E. Brown took over the Grand Hotel, and in May she began making renovations, including adding a mansard room, which had two slopes on all sides, with the lower slope steeper than the upper one. That addition caused some problems in town, which included dirt and debris in the street and concerns that this new roof was a fire hazard. While contractors were building a second story for the Grand Hotel that included five patented fire escapes, Brown visited San Francisco to purchase the necessary furniture for the addition. Even the notorious "Cowboys" were impressed with the Grand's accommodations, and they frequently stayed there. The guest register often included Ike Clanton, Phineas Clanton, Billy Clanton, and Johnny Ringo. Jessie Brown also ensured that her patrons' eating needs were met and in September asked Henry Holthower to run the Grand Hotel's dining room. Holthower, the former cook at the Can Can Restaurant, had a legal issue with Brown in December and left.

THE GRAND HOTEL, TOMBSTONE.

This fine property, on Allen street, between Fourth and Fifth streets, is quite an ornament to the city; it

till their pinnacles h
have melted into vall
solid silver, sands ye
beside which those

The Grand Hotel, circa 1880
ARIZONA QUARTERLY ILLUSTRATED, 1880

On January 13, 1882, the Grand Hotel was acquired by Archie McBride; his wife, Frances "Fannie"; and Cochise County's sheriff, John Behan. The newlywed McBrides spared no expense in making it a truly "grand" hotel and visited a furniture manufacturer in St. Louis, Missouri, to make their purchases. When former owner Jessie Brown departed for New Mexico, she left the hotel empty and in a state of disarray, so the McBrides had to start anew. Mrs. McBride was also involved in the Grand's new look, and while her husband was busying himself with the furniture delivery, she placed plants near the windows of each hall on the upper floor of the hotel. The porch on the second floor was also ornamented with ivies and other climbers that eliminated empty spaces between the windows.

GRAND HOTEL.

Bill of Fare for Sunday, Oct. 23d. 4,30 p. m. Tough Nut Time.

SOUP.

Chicken Giblet.

FISH.

Salmon, Egg Sauce.

BOILED.

Beef, Herb Sauce.

ROAST.

Chicken, Mushroom Sauce. Pork, Beef.

ENTREES.

Chicken Potpie,
Beef a la Mode,
Chicken Giblets,
Ham, Champagne Sauce,
Apple Fritters, Wine Sauce.

VEGETABLES.

Sweet Potatoes,
Mashed Potatoes,
Turnips,
Corn.

PASTRY.

Currant and Blackberry Pie,
Ice Cream and Cake.

The Grand's menu offered a multitude of dining options.
TOMBSTONE DAILY NUGGET, OCTOBER 23, 1881

An *Epitaph* reporter was given a tour of the newly renovated hotel. He reported: "One cannot help but smile on entering the handsome parlor, the scene which greets the eye is so pleasing. This apartment has been furnished in red, according to the latest style, and is really beautiful. In fact, the neatness in all the furniture, the bright pretty designs of the carpets, make all the rooms appear so cozy that you want to move right in." Even Isaac "Ike" Clanton spent a night in the newly renovated hotel. The McBrides also converted an unoccupied store space in the hotel into the dining room, where delicious meals were served by Messrs. Frazer and DeGraw.

In April, Archie McBride fell ill with a "congestive chill," and Fannie McBride hired Julian Piercy of Prescott, Arizona, to manage things while the couple traveled to Yuma, Arizona, so that Archie could recover. Upon their return, Archie went back to work and designed a separate room in the hotel for meetings of the Tombstone Club that offered billiards and chess. They held a huge reception so attendees could marvel at the richly wall-papered walls, lush Brussels carpets, and elegant furnishings. Refreshments were served at eleven-thirty during a break from the dance floor. Some of the original members of the club included John Behan, Milton Joyce, John Dunbar, Harry Woods, Ward Priest, Richard Rule, E. B. Gage, and Dr. George Goodfellow.

The McBride's Grand Hotel was doing great, but Archie never really recovered from his illness. On May 15, 1882, he died of consumption, and his bereaved new bride Fannie was left to manage the hotel along with silent partner John Behan. Ten days later the hotel and restaurant were destroyed in a fire. The hotel never reopened, but the restaurant did.

LOBSTER SALAD ❧

Imported goods were used to make trendy dishes that were made possible because of the variety of supplies that arrived in Tombstone via freighters, which brought in goods on a regular basis as early as 1880. Goods came from everywhere imaginable, including California, the East Coast, Asia, and Europe. The variety of ingredients available to local restaurants and home cooks included ham from the Westphalian region of Germany, molasses from Louisiana, and tea from Japan. When H. E. Hills and Company opened in late 1880 at 217 4th Street, they advertised extracted honey, Japanese tea, deep-sea codfish, New Orleans molasses, and lobster. This recipe was adapted from the *Tombstone Epitaph*, August 2, 1890.

SERVES 2

2 cups finely chopped cooked lobster

¼ teaspoon freshly ground pepper

¼ cup mayonnaise

¼ teaspoon salt, if needed

¼ cup lettuce

Place all the ingredients except the lettuce in a bowl; combine well. Serve on a bed of lettuce.

RUSS HOUSE

Sol T. Anderson and Jacob Smith opened the Russ House, a boardinghouse with a first-class saloon, at the end of 1880. It sat on the corner of 5th and Toughnut Streets, directly opposite the entrance to some of Tombstone's earliest mines. The *Tombstone Epitaph* described the Russ House as a first-class adobe building with a wide veranda that faced both streets, where customers could see the workings of the mines. The dining room was one of the largest in Tombstone, and the kitchen had a new range to prepare the meals. Their chef was Edward Rafferty, who was well known in the business and once owned the Miner's Restaurant. The Russ House also had a first-class saloon, with Charles Stuart, recently from Eureka, Nevada, behind the bar. The paper reported: "All in all, it is a handsome establishment, and is deserving of a liberal patronage." Single meals cost 50 cents, and room and board was $2.50 per day.

In October 1881 Joseph Pascholy partnered with Nellie Cashman to take over the management and ownership. The *Epitaph* reported: "The homelike features of the Russ House will be appreciated in a land where homes are scarce, and where bachelors are unpleasantly numerous." Under this management, the Russ House Hotel served its first dinner on October 3; more than 400 people dined. Even though the business was prospering, just one month after opening, Cashman announced that she would be selling her interest in the Russ House for personal reasons. It would not, however, be the end of Cashman's association with the Russ House. Nellie left the Russ House in April 1882, but it continued to thrive under the direction of Pascholy. She left to open the American House with her sister, Frances Cunningham.

In 1883 Pascholy sold the Russ House back to Nellie and her sister so he could open the Occidental Hotel. In 1884 Nellie Cashman sold the Russ House and its contents to her sister, Fannie Cunningham, and Kate Ward for $3,500. Her well-stocked pantry included cases of oysters, fresh squash, salmon, salt, coconut cakes, lard, port wine, raisins, barrels of beer, 100 pounds rice, ½ barrel vinegar, 20 dozen bottles whiskey, 8 gallons catsup, grapes, 2½ barrels mackerel, 500 pounds dried apples, 60 pounds dried corn, 7 gallons brandy, 2 barrels blackberry brandy, and 500 pounds ham. The sale included flavoring extracts, macaroni, yeast, canned pie fruits, and spices. Unfortunately, her sister succumbed to tuberculosis and Cashman became mother to Cunningham's five young children along with a very large business to manage by herself. In August 1884, Mrs. Annie B. Paddock leased the Russ House.

Chapter Three

THE MAIN EVENT: ENTREES

Menus in Tombstone included selections from soup to nuts. Several categories that we would call entrees today fell under the headings of Boiled, Entrees, Roasts, Fish, and Relieves/Relishes. Many included trendy French sauces; wild game meats like rabbit, venison, and antelope; and imported items like ham and oysters, as well as meats from local butchers.

BEEF À LA MODE ✌

French food was very trendy in the 1880s, and certain cooking terms may seem misleading. Before you pass on this recipe, let me assure you that none of the ingredients include ice cream. "À la mode" simply means "on the top." Many ingredients, like ketchup, had to be made and were not readily available like they are today. This recipe was adapted from *Mrs. Beeton's Dictionary of Every-day Cookery.*

SERVES 4–6

4-pound round roast

8 pieces salt pork or bacon

¼ teaspoon salt

¼ teaspoon freshly ground pepper

½ cup flour

4 tablespoons butter

⅓ cup diced celery

⅓ cup diced turnip

⅓ cup diced carrots

⅓ cup diced onion

1 bay leaf

2 sprigs parsley

1 cup white wine

1 tablespoon ketchup

Water, enough to halfway cover roast

4 tablespoons butter

4 tablespoons flour

Using a knife, make 8 horizontal slits in the meat. Push the pieces of salt pork or bacon into the slits. Season the meat with the salt and pepper, and then dredge through the flour. In a large Dutch oven, melt the butter over medium heat. Brown the roast on all sides.

Add the remaining ingredients to the pan except the 4 tablespoons of flour and butter. Be sure to put everything around the roast, not *on* it. Cover and cook over low heat for 4 hours. Do not allow the water to boil. When the roast is tender, remove and place on a serving platter. Strain the liquid and set it aside.

In the same pan, melt the additional 4 tablespoons of butter; add the 4 tablespoons of flour and cook for 3 to 4 minutes, or until golden. Gradually add the reserved liquid and whisk for 5 minutes, or until thick. Season with salt and pepper to taste. Pour the gravy over the roast, or serve it on the side.

TOMBSTONE'S BUTCHERS

In 1881 Tombstone's butchering industry saw big changes, and the firm of Hooker and Bauer ended. Henry Clay Hooker's son Edward opened a butcher shop on Allen, and the following month Apollinar Bauer sold his 160-acre ranch near the Dragoon Mountains to his brother Bernard. He later sold his butchering business to Jacob Everhardy, who named it the Fremont Street Market. Bauer went into a new line of work for a while, using his own driving team to haul adobe and sand for the local masons. After Bernard opened a butcher shop in the fall, Apollinar worked for him. Bernard and James Kehoe partnered to open the Union Poultry and Meat Market at Apollinar's old location. Their business did well, and they purchased 600 head of American cattle from Mr. E. B. Frink in the Sulphur Springs Valley. Bauer and Kehoe reportedly had one of the "neatest" delivery wagons in Tombstone.

On February 12 the Territory of Arizona enacted a law that regulated the butchering business to help reduce cattle rustling and protect ranchers. The law stated that anyone who butchered or slaughtered horned cattle was required to follow certain regulations, including keeping a record book that described each animal; its brand, age, and weight; and the person from whom the animal was purchased. It also required a butcher to file a $1,000 bond with the county and to keep the animal's hide available for inspection for ten days from the slaughter date so the animal's brand could be identified. If a butcher failed to comply, he would be charged with a misdemeanor and, if convicted, subject to a fine from $10 to $100 for each offense.

Butchers were not the only ones in the cattle business affected by the new laws. Some of the other regulations addressed cattle theft, the driving of stolen cattle, rustling, and the sale of stolen cattle, all of which were considered grand larceny and punishable by spending one to ten years in the territorial prison in Yuma, Arizona. However, a rustler in those days probably would have preferred spending time in jail rather than have a disgruntled rancher punish him, which may have involved a rope necktie!

STRIP STEAK ✦

In 1881 John Grattan was the proprietor of the Bon Ton Restaurant. His bill of fare was extensive and included soup, fish, entrees, roasts, and vegetables. He also offered three other categories: Eggs; "General," which included breakfast items; and "Cooked to Order." Items in that category included mutton chop, sausage, fried ham, pork chop, liver and bacon, porterhouse steak, rib steak, beefsteak, and sirloin steak. This recipe was adapted from the *Arizona Sentinel*, June 2, 1888.

SERVES 1–2

1- to 1½-inch-thick, 6- to 8-ounce strip steak

1 tablespoon olive oil

Salt and pepper to taste

Rosemary sprig

3 tablespoons butter

Allow steak to sit at room temperature for 20–30 minutes; rub with salt and pepper. Heat olive oil in a cast iron skillet over medium-high heat; add the meat with some rosemary. Allow to cook on one side for about 3 minutes. Once the meat releases itself from the pan, turn it over. Allow to cook for about 5 minutes, or until it reaches 125°F, for medium-rare. Remove the steak from the pan before cutting. Add the butter to the skillet and scrape the pan until the butter melts. Pour melted butter over the steak.

O.K. CORRAL GUNFIGHT

October 26, 1881, was a cold and snow-flurried day that turned deadly. City Marshal Virgil Earp, along with his brothers Wyatt and Morgan and their close friend John "Doc" Holliday, faced the "Cowboys," who included the Clantons and the McLaurys. When the shooting stopped and the smoke cleared, three were dead and three were injured. Judge Wells Spicer, who presided over the hearing, stated that Virgil Earp, as chief of police, Morgan and Wyatt Earp, and Doc Holliday, who Virgil called upon for help, went to the site of the fight, near the O.K. Corral, for the purpose of arresting and disarming the Clantons and McLaurys. Spicer did feel there was enough evidence to support a trial. Although the fight was between the Earps, Holliday, the Clantons, and the McLaurys, it affected the entire town. Wyatt Earp and Holliday were eventually arrested, and a lengthy hearing ensued. After their arrest, the judge set their bail at $20,000 each. Many of the businessmen in town were friends with the Earps and Holliday and showed their support by rallying together to raise the needed money. Some of those businessmen included Charley Brown, owner of Brown's Hotel, and Albert Bilicke, owner of the Cosmopolitan Hotel.

ROAST BEEF ✌

Bauer's meat market was a popular place for shopping, but it also played a role in the gunfight hearings. On October 26, 1881, dressmaker Mrs. M. J. King was in Bauer's meat market at the time of the shooting. While she was choosing what meat to buy, she heard several gunshots. She later testified that she had witnessed Holliday and the Earps passing by while she was in Bauer's shop. This recipe was adapted from *One Thousand and One Useful Recipes and Valuable Hints About Cooking and Housekeeping*.

SERVES 4–6

4- to 6-pound eye round roast

2 tablespoons salt

1 teaspoon freshly ground pepper

½ cup flour

Preheat oven to 450°F. Rinse roast and pat dry. Rub salt and pepper on all sides of the roast. Dredge the seasoned roast in the flour. Allow to sit, uncovered, in the refrigerator for 1 hour or up to 72 hours.

Remove the roast from the refrigerator and allow to rest for 30 minutes. Place the roast on a baking rack or in a roasting pan. Cook the meat uncovered at 450°F for 15 minutes. Reduce the heat to 250°F and cook for 1–2 hours for a medium roast. The internal temperature should read 130°F–140°F for medium-rare. Remember that even after you take the roast from the oven, it will continue to cook for a few more minutes.

Remove the roast and allow it to sit, loosely covered, for 20 minutes before carving.

After removing the roast from the pan, skim any excess fat from the pan juices. Add 1½ cups boiling water to the pan, and scrape the bottom to remove the crusty bits.

Arrange the roast on a serving platter and pour the gravy over it. Garnish with fresh parsley or thyme, and serve with sautéed mushrooms.

RIBS OF BEEF (PRIME RIB)

The threat of a beef shortage in 1881 didn't stop the owners of the Elite Restaurant at 215 Allen from enlarging their restaurant's accommodations. The *Epitaph* reported that the new dining room was one of the largest and best appointed in Arizona. Ribs of beef, or prime rib as we know it today, was served at the Occidental Chop House, Russ House, and Grand Hotel. It was often served with horseradish. This recipe was adapted from *Mrs. Beeton's Dictionary of Every-day Cookery.*

SERVES 6–8

4-pound prime rib

¼ cup kosher salt

2 teaspoons freshly ground pepper

Horseradish

Three days before you plan to roast the meat, salt and pepper it and allow to sit, uncovered, in the refrigerator. This helps age the meat and retain its juices while cooking. Preheat the oven to 250°F and place the roast, fat sit up, in a roaster. Place in oven and cook until center of roast registers 120°F–125°F on an instant-read thermometer for rare, 130°F for medium-rare, or 135°F for medium to medium-well. This will take 3½–4 hours.

When done, remove the roast from the oven and cover loosely with foil. Allow to rest for at least 30 minutes, but no more than an hour. When ready to serve, turn oven to 500°F; uncover the roast and place it in the oven. Roast for 5–10 minutes, until brown and crispy. Remove from oven and slice. Serve with pan juices and horseradish.

VEAL CUTLETS, BREADED ✐

In 1881 Julius Caesar, a 38-year-old native of Hanover, Germany, opened the New York Bakery, Restaurant and Coffee House. He advertised that first-class meals and fresh baked goods could always be procured at 415 Allen Street. He also prepared items for Tombstone's many parties and social functions. In addition to the regular business from his shop, Caesar supplemented his income by preparing meals for Tombstone's prisoners. At the end of each month, Caesar submitted a bill to the city marshal or city council for reimbursement. This recipe was adapted from San Francisco's *Daily Examiner*, April 9, 1887.

SERVES 4

1 pound veal cutlets, ⅛ inch thick

½ teaspoon salt

¼ teaspoon freshly ground pepper

5 tablespoons butter

⅓ cup flour

½ teaspoon each, dried thyme and rosemary

2 eggs, lightly beaten

1 cup dry breadcrumbs

2 tablespoons butter

2 tablespoons flour

½ cup water or white wine

1 teaspoon lemon juice

Lemon slices

Season the cutlets with the salt and pepper. Place the flour and herbs, eggs, and breadcrumbs in three separate bowls or pie plates.

Dredge the veal in the herb flour, then the eggs, and finally the breadcrumbs. Melt 3 tablespoons of butter in a heavy-duty skillet and heat over medium-high heat. Gently place the cutlets in the skillet and cook until browned.

If you cannot cook the cutlets all at once, place the cooked ones in a covered dish and keep in a 250°F oven while you cook the rest.

When done cooking all the cutlets, add the remaining butter and melt over medium heat; stir in the flour and cook for 1 minute. Add enough water or wine to make a slightly thick sauce. Add the lemon juice and pour over the cutlets. Serve on a platter garnished with lemon slices.

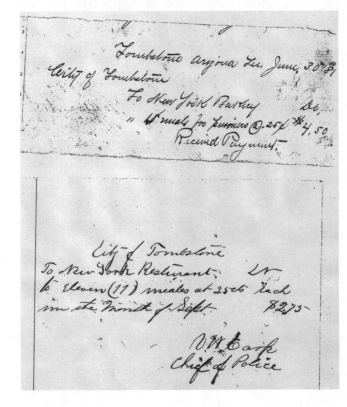

Julius Caesar presented this bill to Chief of Police Virgil Earp on June 30, 1881, for prisoner meals made at his New York Bakery and Restaurant.

ARIZONA HISTORICAL SOCIETY

VEAL CUTLETS, PLAIN ❧

Tombstone's mines were generating a fortune in 1881, and the town bustled with surveyors, barbers, tailors, newspapermen, doctors, attorneys, saloonkeepers, and restaurateurs. It now had three water companies and gas lighting to illuminate its approximately twenty-four restaurants, which did not include the lunch stands in the saloons. Two of those restaurants were the Nevada Restaurant at 605 Allen Street, run by former Virginia City, Nevada, resident E. H. Jackson, and the Brooklyn Restaurant at 525 Allen, run by Captain John S. Young. Young was the mayor of Virginia City in 1872 and was murdered in New Mexico in 1882. Imagine sitting down to a dish like this in one of those restaurants. This recipe was adapted from San Francisco's *Daily Examiner*, April 9, 1887.

SERVES 4

1 pound veal cutlets, 1 inch thick

¼ teaspoon salt

⅛ teaspoon freshly ground pepper

1 tablespoon butter

½ tablespoon oil

½ cup dry white wine

½ teaspoon thyme

1 tablespoon butter, cut into pieces

Note: If you prefer not to use veal, use pork, chicken, or even venison.

Wash and dry the cutlets; season with salt and pepper. Melt 1 tablespoon butter and the oil in a large frying pan. Cook the cutlets over medium-high heat for 5–6 minutes on each side. Remove the cutlets and place on a serving platter. Deglaze the pan with the wine. Add the thyme and cook for 5 minutes to reduce. Remove from the heat and whisk in the butter pieces. Pour the sauce around the veal cutlets and serve.

HAM WITH CHAMPAGNE SAUCE ❧

Cooked ham could be used in many ways, and this recipe shows its French influence with the champagne sauce. It's especially frugal as a means to dress up leftover ham and was often served at the Russ House and Occidental Chop House. If you are using leftovers, skip to the champagne sauce. This recipe was adapted from California's *Placer Herald*, May 29, 1880.

SERVES 4–6

5- to 7-pound ham

½ cup brown sugar

3 tablespoons mustard

½ cup white wine

Champagne Sauce
(recipe follows)

Place the ham in a baking pan, fat side up. Mix the brown sugar, mustard, and wine in a small bowl. Spread over the ham, reserving some of the mixture. Bake at 350°F for 3½ hours, basting occasionally with the sugar mixture. Check with a meat thermometer to ensure doneness. Slice the ham and serve with champagne sauce.

CHAMPAGNE SAUCE ❧

MAKES 2 CUPS

---

1 tablespoon butter

1 tablespoon flour

1 cup beef stock

½ cup champagne

Salt and pepper to taste

Melt the butter in a large saucepan over medium heat; add the flour and cook until it starts to brown but not burn. Gradually add the stock and cook until slightly thickened. Add the champagne and heat through. Season to taste with salt and pepper.

PORK CUTLETS WITH SAUCE ROBERT ❧

When this dish appeared on the Occidental Chop House's menu in 1881, it was printed in French as *Cotellets D'cochon*, Sauce Robert. This restaurant's talented chef was Alvan S. Young, but his tenure as cook was temporary. His early departure was also prompted by the fact that Young had been involved in a fight at the restaurant. He was quickly replaced when his predecessor, a French chef named Louis Rich, came back to Tombstone from a summer sojourn in Hermosillo, Mexico. This recipe was adapted from *Mrs. Beeton's Dictionary of Everyday Cookery*.

SERVES 4

4–6 pork cutlets, ½ inch thick

1 tablespoon butter

1 tablespoon oil

½ onion, minced

1 cup dry white wine

2 cups beef stock

3 tablespoons Dijon mustard

2 tablespoons chopped parsley

Sauté the cutlets in the butter and oil over medium-high heat in a large skillet until they are no longer red inside, about 15 minutes. Remove the cutlets and place on a serving platter.

Cook the onions in the skillet for 10 minutes, or until tender. Slowly add the wine and allow it to reduce to about 4 tablespoons. Add the beef stock and simmer for 12 minutes. Remove from the heat and whisk in the mustard and parsley. Pour the sauce around the cutlets and garnish with parsley sprigs.

PORK ROAST WITH APPLESAUCE ✌

Jacob Everhardy was a butcher who offered his patrons a variety of meats that included beef, mutton, pork, sausage, and game. He also offered free delivery to all parts of the city from his shop at 404 Fremont Street. Chefs at the Grand Hotel, Russ House, Maison Doree, and Occidental Chop House bought pork and served this dish, which was adapted from the *Weekly Louisiana Review*, February 13, 1889. The applesauce recipe was adapted from San Francisco's *Daily Examiner*, July 19, 1885.

SERVES 4–6

3- to 4-pound boneless pork roast

¼ teaspoon freshly ground pepper

½ teaspoon salt

¼ cup flour

Applesauce (recipe follows)

Sprinkle roast with the salt and pepper. Next, dredge it in the flour. Place the pork in a roasting pan, fat side up. Allow to rest in the refrigerator for 1 hour or up to 24. Remove from the refrigerator and allow to sit for 20 minutes. Bake uncovered for 2–2½ hours at 325°F. A meat thermometer should register 145°F when the roast is done. Allow to stand, loosely covered, for 15 minutes before serving. Serve with applesauce.

APPLESAUCE

MAKES 2 CUPS

---

8 tart apples

1 cup water

⅔ cup sugar

1-inch strip of lemon peel

Peel, core, and chop the apples. Place them in a medium stockpot and add the remaining ingredients. Cover and cook over medium-low heat for 10 minutes. The apples should be very tender when done. Remove the lemon peel and mash the apples.

CHICKEN FRICASSEE 🎋

When residents wanted milk or cream for a recipe like this, they ordered from Antonio Gallardo, who had a ranch on the San Pedro River. He supplied Tombstone with "the best quality milk" at only 60 cents a gallon or 20 cents per quart. The cooks in Tombstone used recipes like this one, adapted from *Mrs. Beeton's Dictionary of Every-day Cookery.*

SERVES 4

4 tablespoons butter

1 teaspoon oil

3-pound chicken, cut into pieces

Salt and pepper

¼ cup chopped parsley

2 onions, quartered

4 tablespoons flour

1 cup dry white wine

2 cups chicken stock

½ pound mushrooms, quartered

½ cup heavy cream

Juice of ½ lemon

Melt the butter and oil in a large stockpot over medium heat. Sprinkle the chicken with salt and pepper and add to the pot. Cook the chicken until it is firm and white. Sprinkle the meat with the parsley and add the onions. Cover the pot and simmer for 10–15 minutes. Uncover and sprinkle the chicken and onions with flour. Turn the chicken to coat evenly. Cook for an additional 15 minutes. Gradually stir in the wine and stock; stir to combine. The chicken should be almost covered. If it's not, add more stock. Cover and simmer for 35 minutes. Add the mushrooms and cream; simmer for an additional 10 minutes. Add the lemon juice. Check the seasoning and adjust if needed. Serve over rice.

JUNE 1881 FIRE

June 22, 1881, proved a fateful month for many in Tombstone, especially for poor Kate Killilea, owner of the Golden Eagle Restaurant. First, on June 6, someone broke into her restaurant, chloroformed her, and stole the $500 she kept under her mattress. Just sixteen days later, she lost her restaurant to the fire. It swept through half the town's newly developed business district and destroyed four blocks of businesses that were located east of 5th Street. The reported loss to the town was approximately $250,000. The Arcade Restaurant, now owned by Julius Albert Koska, and Tasker and Pridham's mercantile store, which suffered a $2,500 loss, were also destroyed in the blaze. Fortunately, they and many others were able to rebuild quickly. Tasker and Pridham had no plans to leave Tombstone and signed a ninety-nine-year lease with the Mountain Maid Mining Company to occupy their existing location at the corner of 5th and Allen Streets. Kate Killilea's dreams went up in smoke that day, and she was forced to leave town.

Almost as quickly as the fire destroyed Tombstone, it was rebuilt, despite the fact that most businesses were uninsured. The smoldering remains of the business district were cleared away, and construction of new buildings began shortly after the ground had cooled. In fact, only a month after the fire, half the destroyed business district had been rebuilt. Some businesses were able to rebuild at their old locations; others relocated elsewhere in the city. Despite Tombstone's tremendous losses, it went on to have some of the best businesses and eating establishments a city could offer.

The mercantile store of Cadwell and Stanford was also rebuilt. Another merchant who had no insurance and lost everything to the fire was John Fitzhenry. However, he was able to quickly reopen his store on June 27 at 6th and Fremont Streets. Peter Marcovich reopened the Queen Chop House and signed a monthly lease with Cadwell and Stanford to occupy the former site of the Star Restaurant at 512 Allen Street for $100 per month, where he offered a variety of meals.

ROAST CHICKEN WITH MUSHROOM SAUCE ✌

Robert and Bridget Campbell's New Orleans Restaurant was spared from the June 1881 fire, but it didn't escape damage. The restaurant's kitchen was crushed when the neighboring adobe wall fell into it. The Campbells were able to settle with their neighbor, who paid them $500 for the damage. Bridget Campbell, who was in the kitchen at the time, was not injured and was reported "fortunate to be around to tend to her usual duties." This recipe was adapted from San Francisco's *Daily Bulletin Supplement*, October 13, 1883.

SERVES 4–6

4-pound chicken

½ teaspoon salt

¼ teaspoon freshly ground pepper

1 small onion, quartered

½ stalk celery

3 sprigs parsley

1 tablespoon butter, softened

Mushroom Sauce (recipe follows)

Sprinkle the inside of the chicken with the salt and pepper. Stuff with the onion, celery, and parsley. Tie up the chicken. Spread the butter all over the bird and place in a roasting pan. Bake at 350°F for 1–1½ hours. Pierce the inside leg of the chicken; if the juices run clear, it's done. Remove the chicken and juices from the pan. Allow the chicken to rest for 15 minutes before carving. Meanwhile, make the mushroom sauce.

MUSHROOM SAUCE ✒

MAKES 2 CUPS

1 cup minced fresh mushrooms

4 tablespoons butter

4 tablespoons flour

2 cups milk

Salt and pepper to taste

Chopped fresh green onions
for garnish

In a medium skillet sauté the mushrooms in butter for 5–10 minutes. Add the flour and cook for 2 minutes. Whisk in the milk and simmer for 5 additional minutes. Season with salt and pepper. Arrange the chicken on a serving platter and pour the sauce over it. Garnish with chopped fresh green onions.

CHICKEN SAUTÉ À LA MARENGO ✒

This recipe was popular all over the frontier and, like many others, has French origins. It was named to celebrate Napoleon Bonaparte's Battle of Marengo in June 1800. The traditional recipe calls for a whole cut-up chicken, topped with a fried egg and buttered toast or croutons. I've modified it for today's preferences, using an adaption of this recipe from California's *Oakland Daily Evening Tribune*, March 25, 1880. This was often featured at the Russ House.

SERVES 4

½ teaspoon salt

⅛ teaspoon freshly ground pepper

¼ cup flour

4–6 boneless chicken breasts or thighs

2 tablespoons butter

2 tablespoons oil

½ onion or 4 shallots, chopped

1 garlic clove, minced

½ cup white wine

1 cup beef broth

½ teaspoon fresh thyme

1 cup chopped tomatoes

1 cup fresh mushrooms, quartered

Fresh parsley for garnish

Mix salt, pepper, and flour together in a shallow dish. Coat the chicken with the seasoned flour.

Melt the butter and oil in a large Dutch oven, add the chicken, and brown over medium-high heat on both sides. Remove chicken and set aside.

Add the onions and garlic and sauté for 5 minutes; add any leftover seasoned flour and stir to blend. Add the wine, beef broth, thyme, and tomatoes. Add the chicken and simmer for 15 minutes. Chicken should be 165°F internal temperature. Add the mushrooms and cook for an additional 15 minutes. Place the chicken on a serving platter, pour the sauce around it, and garnish with parsley.

CHICKEN CROQUETTES WITH ASPARAGUS POINTS ✑

When Jessie Brown ran the Grand Hotel in 1881, she realized the need to publish its bill of fare in English instead of French. She was one of the first restaurateurs in Tombstone to do it, but others quickly followed suit. For example, this recipe appeared as Croquettes de Vovaille aux Asparagus Points. This recipe, adapted from Marion Harland's *Breakfast, Luncheon and Tea*, 1875, is an example of classic French cooking and a dish the Grand served.

SERVES 4

2 cups minced cooked chicken

1 teaspoon chopped parsley

½ teaspoon salt

¼ teaspoon freshly ground pepper

¼ teaspoon celery seed

¼ teaspoon minced onion

1 cup gravy or White Sauce (see recipe on page 83)

1 egg, beaten

Dry breadcrumbs for coating

Oil for frying

Note: This recipe also works well with leftover turkey.

Mix the first six ingredients together in a bowl; stir well. Add enough of the white sauce to moisten the mixture, but do not allow it to become too soft. Form the mixture into desired shapes such as cones, balls, cylinders, etc. Gently roll the shapes in the beaten egg and then the breadcrumbs.

Add enough oil to come up about an inch in a frying pan and heat over medium-high heat. Gently place the croquettes in the hot oil and cook until they are golden brown. Drain on a towel.

Arrange croquettes on a serving platter and serve with asparagus points. Asparagus points are simply the tips of the plant that have been prepared in the same manner as the asparagus recipe found on page 102.

CHICKEN POTPIE ✎

Inexpensive to make and easily transportable, potpies were a popular dish in Tombstone at restaurants for miners, and were often featured at charity events. Some recipes called for two traditional piecrusts; others were simply covered with a biscuit or puff pastry topping. This recipe, adapted from California's *Lompoc Record*, February 3, 1877, includes a double piecrust, but feel free to use any type of crust.

SERVES 6–8

---

1 chicken, cooked and deboned

2 tablespoons butter

2 tablespoons flour

¾ teaspoon salt

½ teaspoon freshly ground pepper

2 cups chicken stock

1 double piecrust (see recipe on page 154)

Cut the chicken into bite-size pieces. Place the butter in a large stockpot and cook over low heat until the butter has melted. Add the flour and cook for 2 minutes, stirring constantly. Add the salt, pepper, and chicken stock; stir until slightly thickened. Remove from the heat. Add chicken pieces.

Line a deep-dish pie pan with the first crust and pour the chicken mixture in. Cover with the second crust. Bake at 350°F for 30–40 minutes, or until crust is golden. Allow to sit for about 15 minutes before serving.

1881 MAISON DOREE

Maison Doree, which loosely translates to "house of gold" or "golden house" in French, was originally called the Cosmopolitan Hotel Dining Room in 1880. In 1881 George C. Marks was running the newly named Maison Doree, and Isaac "Little Jakey" Jacobs was in charge of the kitchen. Despite running a successful business, George Marks sold the Maison Doree to Louis Riche and Constantine Protopsaltis, a 20-year-old native of Greece, in December 1881. Riche and Protopsaltis advertised that their new restaurant offered imported and game lunches, eastern oysters, and coffee, bread, and cold meat. They kept their restaurant open until 1:00 a.m. to appease the late-night crowd. They also made improvements over the next few months, supplied "all the market affords," and brought in new furniture and silver forks, knives, and spoons. The *Epitaph* reported: "The cook is one of the most competent in the profession." After Marks sold the Maison Doree, its chef, "Little Jakey," left and took over the Grand Restaurant.

The restaurant briefly closed for repairs and improvements and reopened May 3, 1882. The newspaper noted it was the handsomest restaurant in town and was using silver forks, knives, and spoons. The report also noted that their cook was one of the most competent in his field. At the end of the month, the hotel and restaurant were destroyed in a fire and never reopened.

STUFFED TURKEY ✣

In 1881 grocer John Fitzhenry placed a notice in the newspaper advertising that he had just received a "fine lot of dressed turkeys from Kansas and a large invoice of Booth's Baltimore oysters." His notice also advised that "all judicious and economical housekeepers will find it to their advantage to call as early as possible, as these luxuries are in great demand, being the finest ever brought to this place." The newspapers were filled with advertisements of Thanksgiving items and dinner, but the most notable Thanksgiving dinner event occurred at the Tombstone Engine Company, which gave a "ball supper." The Maison Doree's owner, George Marks, made the occasion especially festive by having menus printed on satin. A writer must have attended the festivities, because on the following day the *Epitaph* reported that Chef Jacobs had served a "daisy dinner." This recipe was adapted from California's *Napa County Reporter*, April 29, 1881.

SERVES 8–10

12- to 14-pound turkey

Stuffing (recipe follows)

4 tablespoons butter, softened

Salt and pepper

2 celery stalks

1 onion, quartered

Preheat oven to 325°F. Remove excess fat from the cavity of the bird and discard. Set the giblets and neck aside. Pat the turkey dry inside and out. Loosely fill the cavity and the neck with the stuffing. Once stuffed, tie up the neck area then the cavity. Before cutting your string, be sure to wrap the legs as well.

Place the turkey in a large roasting pan. Rub the butter all over the bird and sprinkle with 1 teaspoon each of salt and pepper. Place the neck, giblets (the liver is optional), celery, and onion in the bottom of the roasting pan.

Roast uncovered for 15–20 minutes, or until golden, then cover tightly with the lid or foil. Remove the cover 30 minutes before cooking time is up to obtain a crispy, golden skin. A bird this size should take approximately 3½–4 hours to cook. A thermometer can be placed into the fleshy part of a thigh (close to but not touching bone). When it registers 180°F, it's done. You also can stick a fork in the inside leg area; if the juices run clear, the turkey is done.

STUFFING ✐

MAKES ENOUGH FOR A 12- TO 14-POUND TURKEY

1 cup minced onion

1 cup minced celery

½ teaspoon thyme

1 teaspoon sage

4 cups homemade croutons

2 large eggs, lightly beaten

Salt and pepper to taste

Sauté onions and celery over medium heat for 7 minutes, or until tender. Mix in the remaining ingredients and blend well. Allow to cool and then stuff the turkey.

TURKEY HASH WITH DROPPED EGGS ✥

Hash was a frugal way to use leftovers and extend ingredients. As Tombstone residents were winding down from their holiday celebrations, they pondered what to do with leftover turkey, just as we do today. This dish was popular in Tombstone and was often found on bills of fare after Thanksgiving and Christmas. Dropped eggs are poached eggs—sometimes also called whirled eggs. This recipe was adapted from the *Arizona Sentinel*, January 11, 1890.

SERVES 2–4

2 teaspoons butter

¼ cup diced onion or celery

2 cups chopped cooked turkey

¼ teaspoon salt

¼ teaspoon freshly ground pepper

¼–½ cup gravy to moisten the mix

1 tablespoon chopped parsley

Melt the butter over medium heat and add the onion or celery. Cook for about 7 minutes, or until tender. Add the turkey, salt and pepper, and gravy and heat through. Turn the hash onto a serving platter and top with dropped or fried eggs.

Note: Any meat will work with this recipe.

DROPPED EGGS (POACHED) ✥

MAKES 4

1 teaspoon salt

½ teaspoon vinegar

4 eggs

Add the salt and vinegar to a large saucepan of water and bring to a boil. Reduce heat to simmer. Swirl the water, gently break the eggs into the water, and simmer for 3 minutes. Drain the eggs and set on hash. If serving for breakfast, place eggs on toast.

LAMB CUTLETS, BREADED ✺

Otto Geisenhofer was in his new building for less than a year when the June 1881 fire destroyed it. The City Bakery didn't stand a chance of survival, since the fire started only a couple stores away in the Arcade Saloon. Geisenhofer was able to rebuild his business, and the *Epitaph* acknowledged his reopening by stating that his food would be "just as palatable as before he was burned out." This recipe was adapted from San Francisco's *Daily Examiner*, May 29, 1881.

SERVES 2–4

---

4 lamb chops

½ teaspoon salt

¼ teaspoon freshly ground pepper

1 cup dry breadcrumbs

2 eggs, beaten

Oil or butter for frying

Wash and pat the chops dry. Sprinkle both sides with salt and pepper. Dredge the chops through the breadcrumbs, into the eggs, and then back through the breadcrumbs. Fry in ½ inch of hot oil until golden brown on both sides, about 20 minutes. Pierce chops with a fork to see if the juices run clear. Serve with baked macaroni and cheese and sugar peas.

BOILED LEG OF LAMB WITH OYSTER SAUCE 🍂

New restaurants continued to open in 1881 and included Mrs. M. V. Gleason's Fremont Street Restaurant and James McGrath's Mack's Chop House. Austrian cook John Bogovich and his partner, M. Bruce, opened the Rockaway Oyster House at 207 5th Street. The businessmen's first advertisement tantalized readers' palates with items such as fresh fish, chicken, and, of course, oysters, which were offered raw, stewed, or fried—or made into a delicious sauce to accompany lamb. This recipe was adapted from *Mrs. Beeton's Dictionary of Every-day Cookery*.

SERVES 4–6

5-pound leg of lamb

Water

Salt

Oyster Sauce (recipe follows)

Place the lamb in a large Dutch oven. Add enough cold water (be sure to measure it) to cover the lamb. Remove the lamb and add to the Dutch oven 1½ teaspoons of salt for every 4 cups of water you added. Bring this to a boil.

Return the lamb to the boiling water and allow it to come back to a low boil. Reduce the heat to medium and cook for 1½ hours, or until a meat thermometer registers 160°F (well done). Remove lamb from the water and allow to rest for 20 minutes before serving.

Slice the lamb and arrange it on a serving platter. Pour the oyster sauce around the slices.

OYSTER SAUCE ✑

MAKES 2 CUPS

2 pints oysters

½ cup butter

½ cup flour

2 cups milk

¼–½ cup reserved
oyster liquor

½ teaspoon salt

¼ teaspoon freshly
ground pepper

Wash and shuck the oysters, being sure to reserve the oyster liquor. Strain the oyster liquor and set aside.

Melt the butter in a deep frying pan over medium heat. Once the butter has melted, add the flour and cook for 3 minutes. Whisking constantly, gradually pour in the milk and oyster liquor; stir well. Add the salt, pepper, and oysters. Allow this to cook until the edges of the oysters begin to curl. Remove from heat and serve.

VENISON STEAK WITH CLARET JELLY SAUCE ❧

Robert "Bob" Campbell, a 28-year-old Irish immigrant, along with his wife, Bridget, opened the New Orleans Restaurant and Liquor Saloon at 219 4th Street in 1881, next to Joseph Stumpf's American Bakery. Restaurants like the New Orleans had standing orders for fresh game from local hunters when it was available, and it was a real treat for Tombstonians when restaurants offered it. This recipe was adapted from the New Orleans, Louisiana, *Daily Picayune*, November 26, 1882.

SERVES 4

---

4 venison steaks, ½ inch thick

Salt and pepper

Claret Jelly Sauce (recipe follows)

Add salt and pepper to the steaks and allow to rest for about 5 minutes. Brush with oil, and broil or grill the steaks over medium-high heat for 7–10 minutes, or until desired doneness is reached. Place on a serving platter and serve with jelly sauce.

Note: If the venison is wild and not farm-raised, you may want to soak it overnight in salted water or milk before cooking. This will remove some of the gaminess.

CLARET JELLY SAUCE ✌

MAKES 2 CUPS

1 cup beef stock

1 teaspoon salt

½ teaspoon freshly ground pepper

Dash of cayenne

2 cloves

3 dried allspice berries

2 tablespoons butter

1 teaspoon flour

1 teaspoon currant jelly

1 cup claret wine

Combine the stock and the seasonings in a saucepan; bring to a boil. Mix the butter and flour into a paste, then combine with the jelly and claret. Add the mixture to the stock in the saucepan and bring to a boil again. Remove from the heat; strain.

ROAST VENISON WITH APPLESAUCE ❧

Some of the larger restaurants placed their bills of fare in the newspapers, but most of the other restaurants either ran small ads or did not advertise at all. The bills of fare also listed meal prices, which ranged from 25 to 50 cents. Whether that price was reasonable or expensive depended on what one did for a living. Restaurant proprietors realized that many patrons worked odd hours, so many of them provided meals at all hours of the day and night. Other restaurants kept to the traditional scheduled dinner hours, much as we do today. The other reason that not all restaurants were open day and night was the cost of business licenses, which were more expensive for those who opted to keep their restaurants open continuously. Wild game, like venison, was wildly popular when it could be had. This recipe was adapted from *Mrs. Beeton's Dictionary of Every-day Cookery*.

SERVES 4–6

3- to 4-pound venison roast

2 tablespoons butter to rub the roast

½ teaspoon salt

¼ teaspoon pepper

½ teaspoon dried thyme

3 tablespoons butter

1 onion, sliced

Applesauce (see recipe on page 57)

Rub the roast with the butter, salt, pepper, and thyme. Melt the additional 3 tablespoons butter in a frying pan; add the roast, and sauté over medium-high heat for 3–4 minutes. Set aside and cover.

Place the roast and onions in a roasting pan; cover. Place in a 325°F oven and bake for about 2½ hours, or until tender. Serve with the pan juices and a side of applesauce.

Note: If your venison is not farm-raised, it may need to be soaked overnight in salt water to help remove some of the gaminess. Place the meat in a glass dish, and add enough water to cover the meat. Add 1 teaspoon salt for each 1 quart water. Refrigerate and soak overnight. Rinse, and the meat is ready to be cooked.

RABBIT SAUTÉ À LA CHASSEUR ✑

The Maison Doree restaurant served trendy French dishes to Tombstonians; items included salmon croquettes, chicken liver patties with Madeira sauce, and this dish, whose recipe was adapted from Salt Lake City's *Daily Tribune*, November 10, 1900.

SERVES 4

3 tablespoons flour

1 teaspoon fresh thyme

½ teaspoon salt

¼ teaspoon freshly ground pepper

1-pound rabbit, quartered

3 tablespoons bacon fat

½ pound mushrooms, sliced

¼ cup minced shallots

1 cup diced tomatoes

¼ teaspoon salt

⅛ teaspoon freshly ground pepper

½ cup red wine

¼ cup beef stock

Chopped fresh parsley

Note: If you can't get rabbit, try using game hens or chicken thighs.

Combine the flour, thyme, salt, and pepper in a small bowl. Coat the rabbit with the seasoned flour. Next, melt 3 tablespoons bacon fat over medium-high heat in a large frying pan. Once the fat has melted, add the rabbit and sauté until golden brown on all sides. Remove from pan.

Sauté the mushrooms in the melted fat for 5 minutes over medium heat; add the shallots and cook for 1 minute more. Add the tomatoes and seasonings. Simmer for 5 minutes. Pour the wine and beef stock over the tomato mixture and boil for 5 minutes, or until the sauce has slightly thickened.

Arrange the rabbit pieces on a serving platter and pour the chasseur sauce over them. Sprinkle with freshly chopped parsley.

ROASTED DUCK ✒

In 1881 Aristotle Petro enhanced his Occidental Chop House by repapering and renovating it and adding a private ladies' dining room in the front. The Occidental's bills of fare were remarkable and specialized in classic French cuisine. Petro himself was very clever when he placed his advertisements in the local newspapers. One ad included this quote from poet John Keats: "A thing of beauty (is) a joy forever." A local paper wrote, "Al racked his brains for new dishes until his hair [began] to fall like the Autumn leaves." This recipe was adapted from the *Weekly Louisiana Review*, January 9, 1889.

SERVES 4

4- to 5-pound duck

1 teaspoon salt

½ teaspoon freshly ground pepper

1 apple, cut in quarters

1 cup currant or cranberry jelly

Preheat oven to 450°F. Season the inside and outside of duck with salt and pepper. Score the duck about ½ inch deep in a cross pattern, but don't go down to the meat. Stuff the apple pieces into the duck.

Place the duck, fat side up, in an uncovered roasting pan, and roast for 15 minutes to crisp the skin. Reduce heat to 350°F and cook for an additional 1½–2 hours, until desired doneness is reached. A well-done duck will take about 2 hours.

Remove duck from the oven and spread the jelly over it; allow to rest, loosely covered, for about 15 minutes. Slice and serve with additional jelly.

ROAST QUAIL ✌

Isaac "Jakey" Jacobs was a 27-year-old Russian whose catering skills were well known. He worked at the Maison Doree, and the restaurant regularly advertised that fresh oysters were always available and that only French-trained cooks were employed. One of Jacobs's many duties was to procure meat for the restaurant, so he placed an ad in the local paper soliciting wild game. Jacobs's appeal to the public worked, and shortly thereafter he was preparing delicious meals for his patrons. He later served George Hearst, father of William Randolph Hearst, when he toured the mines in southern Arizona. This recipe was adapted from California's *Sacramento Daily-Record Union*, March 5, 1881.

SERVES 4–6

6 quail

Butter, softened

1 cup flour

½ teaspoon salt

¼ teaspoon black pepper

Wash the quail inside and out and pat dry. Close the birds by tying the legs together.

Rub butter over the birds and set aside. Combine flour, salt, and pepper in a shallow pan. Dredge the birds in the flour to coat evenly.

Place in a roasting pan and bake uncovered at 350°F for 25 minutes, or until done, basting occasionally with the butter.

OYSTERS IN BATTER ⁓

California distributors often advertised in Tombstone's newspapers to attract the attention of businesses and home cooks alike. Emerson Corville & Co. of San Francisco placed an ad for eastern-transported oysters that were shipped in cans by express and packed in ice. Recipes like this, adapted from Marion Harland's *Breakfast, Luncheon and Tea*, 1875, were often served in town.

SERVES 4

12–24 oysters
(fresh or canned)

¼ teaspoon salt

Dash of freshly
ground pepper

1¼ cups flour

½ cup milk

2 eggs, well beaten

3–6 tablespoons
butter, for frying

Drain the oysters and set aside on paper towels. In a bowl, combine the dry ingredients. Combine the milk and the eggs and blend well. Adjust the milk or flour for preferred batter thickness.

Melt the butter over medium-high heat in a large frying pan.

Dip each oyster into the batter twice; gently place in the pan and cook until golden on both sides. Place on paper towels to drain excess oil. Arrange on a platter and serve immediately.

Ads like this appeared in Tombstone newspapers to inform readers of all the tasty treats being shipped to the businesses in town.
THE *TOMBSTONE EPITAPH*,
FEBRUARY 12, 1882

TOMBSTONE'S FEMALE ENTREPRENEURS

A number of women ran successful businesses in Tombstone. Some came with their husbands, some were searching for riches, and others needed a respectable way to earn a living. One of these was Miss Josie Leary, who ran The Brunswick on Allen Street, near 4th, and sold oysters, ice cream, and general refreshments in 1881. Other female entrepreneurs included Irish native Jennie Harden, owner of the Boss Restaurant at 605 Allen Street in 1882; Mrs. Florence Hemsath, who operated the Bon Ton Restaurant at 321 Fremont; Mrs. Jessie Brown, who was in charge of the Grand Hotel; Mrs. M. R. Christie, proprietor of a lodging house; Mrs. Frances Cunningham of Delmonico Lodgings; and Miss Kate Killilea, owner of the Golden Eagle Restaurant.

One of the few new eating establishments to open in 1883 was George and Sophie Gregor's California Restaurant, at 715 Allen Street. To solicit new business, the Gregors placed an ad in the *Tombstone Republican* that read: "Wanted. Seventy-five able bodied men to board at the California Restaurant."

A stroll down the streets of Tombstone allowed patrons to choose their favorite restaurant and meet the people who made them popular. The American Restaurant was owned by Mrs. S. J. Dill, whose cook, Tom Rains, prepared meals for the city's prisoners. Even though the Brooklyn Restaurant was owned by Joseph A. Bright, he hired Katie Lacy to waitress, and the meals were prepared by Mrs. Maggie McGivney, who was the head cook. The American House was owned by Mrs. H. E. Hanford, who employed Mrs. Love as her housekeeper. Pauline Jones owned the International Restaurant and employed Katy Rafferty, Louise Rollins, and Belle Perry. Mrs. Jane Harding and Catherine Lang remained the proprietresses of the Melrose Restaurant. These ladies employed E. B. Lang, who worked behind the scenes to keep their books in order; Lizzie McCormick waited on customers and kept the dining room running smoothly. Carrie Gregory, one of Tombstone's local thespians, ran Gregory's Restaurant at 410 Fremont; Mrs. L. T. Sewell ran The Nucleus on 5th, between Allen and Fremont; and Mrs. King had her restaurant and lodging house on 4th, four doors from the Occidental Hotel in 1884. The Palace Lodging House had four different female owners; Miss Lucy Young ran it from 1882 to 1884, and Mrs. D. B. Immel had it between 1884 and 1885. The last owner was Pauline Jones's sister, Mrs. Henriette Bastian, who owned it from 1886 until 1894, when she sold it to Mrs. S. Gallen. These women offered delicious meals to their guests and local residents alike.

OYSTER PIE WITH WHITE SAUCE ❧

Fresh fish and oysters were a specialty of the Can Can, and they were well known for their delicious oyster dishes. This one was adapted from Marion Harland's *Breakfast, Luncheon and Tea*, 1875.

MAKES 1 PIE

4 cups medium oysters, fresh (shucked) or canned

2½ cups chicken stock

3 medium potatoes, cubed

2 celery stalks, chopped

1 tablespoon chopped parsley

2 cups White Sauce (recipe follows)

1 double piecrust (see recipe on page 154)

Drain the oysters, reserving the liquor. Place the chicken stock, potatoes, celery, and parsley in a large stockpot and bring to a boil. Cook for about 10 minutes, or until potatoes are tender. While this is cooking, make the white sauce.

Add the oysters to the boiling stock and allow it to return to a boil. Reduce heat and simmer until the edges of the oysters begin to curl. Remove from the heat; add the white sauce and stir. Allow this to cool.

Line the bottom of an 8 x 12-inch baking dish with one piecrust. Fill with the oyster mixture, and cover with the second piecrust. Flute the edges and bake at 375°F for 30 minutes, or until golden.

WHITE SAUCE ❧

MAKES 2 CUPS

4 tablespoons butter

6 tablespoons flour

½ teaspoon salt

¼ teaspoon freshly
ground pepper

2 cups milk

Melt the butter in a medium saucepan over medium heat. When the butter begins to bubble, add the flour and seasonings. Stir and cook for 2–3 minutes to allow the flour to cook. Gradually add the milk, whisking constantly until the sauce thickens.

CAN CAN RESTAURANT

The Can Can was opened at 435 Allen Street by Andrew David Walsh and William W. Shanahan in July 1880. Walsh was an Irish machinist and Shanahan, before partnering with Walsh, was proprietor of the Comstock Saloon on 5th Street. The Can Can was another well-established business operated by its original owners, but it relocated after the business was destroyed by fire. They were now located at the Occidental's old location, 429 Allen Street, in a large multiuse building that included the Alhambra Saloon, which was next to the Crystal Palace saloon building. Walsh and Shanahan continued to operate the Can Can successfully, hiring Henry Henninger, Charles Wilson, and Thomas Wren to serve the meals prepared by cook Henry Holthower. Holthower was previously in the restaurant business when he leased the Grand Hotel Dining Room in late 1881. In 1885 the Can Can Restaurant celebrated five years of operation, and the *Daily Record Epitaph* reported: "The Can Can restaurant is one of the oldest and most reliable restaurants in Tombstone, having been running five years, and A. D. Walsh, the proprietor, is bound to make it the leading eating house of the camp." Another story noted that he was "the oldest restaurant man in Tombstone." Two veteran restaurateurs from California worked at the Can Can. Benjamin Wurtmann, former chief cook at the Pacific Ocean House in Santa Cruz, prepared the meals, while Mr. Woodward, his former coworker at San Francisco's Popular Restaurant, was the steward. Wurtmann was only with the Can Can for a short time, and later that year found him cooking meals at the Russ House for Nellie Cashman. Henry Holthower, the Can Can's former cook, left Tombstone for Aspen, Colorado, which was being touted as the next Tombstone. A few months after he left, Holthower wrote to his old Tombstone friends that Aspen was crowded and overdone. He claimed that nine out of ten miners were broke and advised his friends to stay in Tombstone, where they were far better off.

Of all Tombstone's businesses, the restaurants operated with the least trouble. The Can Can, one of Tombstone's favorites, continued to serve meals, and, unusually, its proprietor did not change until 1887. Andrew Walsh, who had owned the Can Can since 1881, leased the business to John Watson. Watson, who had only been in town since March, was a well-known restaurant man. The paper noted: "The old restaurant stand-by at the Can Can has returned from California and will assume his position in that eating house to-day. Johnny is one of the best caterers in the city, besides being an obliging gentlemanly man." Watson, in keeping with the times, changed the restaurant's fare. The Can Can now offered the choicest steaks, roasted stuffed pig, chops, cutlets, and custard pie. Also available were spring chickens and fresh eggs from Walsh's poultry yards and milk and butter from the Can Can's dairy. Watson displayed his bountiful fare in the show windows of his restaurant for all to see. A. D. Walsh was now focused on running his Can Can in nearby Bisbee, where many of Tombstone's former residents now resided. John Watson sold the Can Can back to Walsh in April 1889 and purchased the Bisbee location. Tombstone's Can Can was managed by Andrew Walsh's son Willie for a short time; a month later he turned it over to his sister, Nellie. The Can Can moved to the corner of 4th and Allen Streets, where the restaurant continued to serve oysters and fresh fish every day. The newspaper noted, "Game as wild as a tornado, chicken as tender as a maiden's heart, ice cream as delicious as a day in June, dessert that would charm the soul of a South-sea Islander, and smiles as bright as the morning sun will be found at the Can Can today."

CAN CAN
Restaurant

ALLEN ST., BET FOURTH & FIFTH.

Oysters and Fish Fresh Every Day.

—

All the Delicacies in Season.

—

Open at All Hours

—

Miss Nellie V. Walsh, Proprietress.

Nellie Walsh ran the Can Can for a while until she got married.
THE *TOMBSTONE EPITAPH*, JULY 6, 1889

Nellie remained the proprietor of the Can Can until the mid-1890s, when her father took over again for a few years. He sold the restaurant to John Henninger in 1897 and moved back to Phoenix to give Nellie away when she got married. The Can Can was one of the few restaurants that had operated continuously since its early beginnings, but it too closed after the turn of the century. It became a dry goods store for a time and was opened up again in 1901 by Henninger. He eventually sold it to Ah Lum and Ah Sing, who called it the American Kitchen.

SALMON AU GRATIN ✌

Salmon was often brought in from the Pacific Northwest, and chefs created a variety of tasty recipes with it. The Can Can and some of Tombstone's larger restaurants, such as the Russ House, the Occidental, the Grand, and the Maison Doree, repeatedly placed bills of fare in the Sunday newspapers. Virgil Earp's wife, Allie, recalled, "The best cafes, like the Maison Doree, Can Can, and Fountain, purred with excellent service to match the cuisine." This recipe was adapted from *Mrs. Beeton's Dictionary of Every-day Cookery.*

SERVES 4–6

---

1 tablespoon butter

½ cup chopped mushrooms

2 tablespoons minced fresh parsley

2 pounds salmon, cut into serving-size pieces

½ teaspoon salt

¼ teaspoon freshly ground pepper

1 cup dry breadcrumbs

¼ teaspoon grated nutmeg

3 tablespoons butter

1 cup sherry or Madeira

Lemons

Butter a baking dish; place half the mushrooms and parsley in the bottom. Season the salmon with salt and pepper and place in the dish. Sprinkle the breadcrumbs on top; season with a little more salt and pepper and the nutmeg. Add the remaining mushrooms and parsley.

Cut the 3 tablespoons butter into pieces and dot the fish with it. Gently pour the sherry over the fish.

Bake for about 20 minutes at 350°F, or until a fork pierces the center of the salmon easily.

If the sauce is too loose, remove the salmon; place the sauce in a pan and bring to a boil to reduce. Serve salmon with sauce and lemon slices.

SALMON, SAUCE HOLLANDAISE ✌

Allie Earp recalled walking along Allen Street with Wyatt's wife, Mattie. They peered at the hotels and restaurants, and she recalled, "We sure slowed down at the Maison Doree and the Can Can, and finally stopped in front of the Occidental to read the menu for Sunday dinner pasted on the window." They saw multiple entries for soup, fish, roasts, cold meats, boiled meats, entrees, and desserts. Mattie said to Allie, "I don't see how nobody could eat all that, but I'd be willin' to try." They didn't eat at public places, so when a "friend" escorted them in a for a meal, they went. Allie recalled, "We were talkin' like that, our mouths waterin', when somebody came up and took us right in. I ain't goin' to say who it was."

Salmon was one of the items on the menu the day Petro served two of the Mrs. Earps! This recipe was adapted from Marion Harland's *Breakfast, Luncheon and Tea*, 1875.

SERVES 2–4

2 pounds salmon, cut into serving-size pieces

½ teaspoon salt

½ teaspoon peppercorns

1 bay leaf

1 slice of onion

1 cup water

1 slice of lemon

1 cup white wine

Dill weed

Hollandaise Sauce
(recipe follows)

Place all the ingredients in a large skillet and simmer, covered, for about 10 minutes. The salmon is done when a fork pierces it easily. Remove salmon from the pan and place on a serving platter. Pour hollandaise sauce over the fish. Garnish with dill weed.

HOLLANDAISE SAUCE ❧

MAKES ½ CUP

2 teaspoons vinegar

1 teaspoon water

2 egg yolks, beaten

½ teaspoon mustard

½ cup butter, cut into pieces

¼ teaspoon salt

Pinch of cayenne pepper

Place vinegar, water, egg yolks, mustard, and one-third of the butter in a medium double boiler. Cook over gently boiling water, stirring constantly, for 2 minutes. Add the second third of the butter and whisk to blend. Once the sauce begins to thicken, add the final third of the butter and whisk to incorporate. Remove sauce from the heat and add the salt and cayenne pepper.

CODFISH, CREME À LA CREME ∾

Grocers like H. E. Hills and Fitzhenry and Mansfield sold to restaurants and hotels, but as more stores opened, customers found competitive prices and a diversity of products. Men like Woodhead and Gay were successful Los Angeles wholesale produce merchants, with stores in several locations, including Phoenix and Tucson. Because of Tombstone's success, they hired Frank N. Wolcott to open a store in town. They often advertised such items as California figs, oranges, nuts, apples, and fresh fish. This recipe was adapted from *Mrs. Beeton's Dictionary of Every-day Cookery.*

SERVES 4

Water

1 slice of lemon

1 teaspoon peppercorns

1 bay leaf

2 pounds codfish

1 tablespoon chopped fresh parsley

1 shallot, chopped

½ teaspoon salt

¼ teaspoon freshly ground pepper

1 cup White Sauce (see recipe on page 83)

½ cup dry breadcrumbs

Add enough water to a large skillet to come up to ½ inch. Add the slice of lemon, a few peppercorns, and the bay leaf. Bring this to a boil. Add the uncooked fish; cover, reduce heat to simmer, and cook for 10 minutes. The fish is done when a fork can easily pierce it. Allow to cool.

Flake the fish with a fork into a small bowl and add the parsley, shallot, salt, and pepper. Gently stir to combine; pour into an ovenproof baking dish. Sprinkle the top with the white sauce and breadcrumbs, and bake at 375°F for 15–20 minutes, or until the top has browned.

Grocers like John Fitzhenry placed ads in newspapers just like grocers do today. This one announced his new coffee grinder, which was a big deal in the 1880s, when people had to grind their own coffee by hand.
THE *TOMBSTONE EPITAPH*, MAY 29, 1881

FRIED FLOUNDER WITH MAÎTRE D'HOTEL SAUCE ✑

"Jakey" Jacobs left the Grand and opened his own restaurant on 4th Street, where he served a "culinary triumph" after one of Tombstone's baseball games in 1882. The dignitaries in attendance were invited to the Cochise Club and then dined at Jakey's, where they enjoyed fresh fish from Guaymas, Sonora, Mexico; oysters from the East; and wild game from the nearby mountains. This recipe was adapted from *Mrs. Beeton's Dictionary of Every-day Cookery.*

SERVES 2–4

2 eggs, beaten

1 cup breadcrumbs

1 pound flounder or sole fillets

Salt and pepper

5 tablespoons butter

1 tablespoon oil

¼ cup butter

¼ cup shallots, diced

½ teaspoon salt

Pinch of freshly ground black pepper

1 teaspoon finely chopped parsley

1 tablespoon lemon juice

Place the beaten eggs and breadcrumbs in separate bowls. Lightly salt and pepper the fillets. Dredge fillets in the eggs and then the breadcrumbs.

Melt the butter and oil over medium-high heat, and begin frying the coated fillets until golden. (If you need to fry in batches, place cooked fillets on a baking sheet and set in a low oven to keep warm.)

Melt the ¼ cup butter in a saucepan and add the shallots. Cook for 3 minutes to soften. Add the salt, pepper, parsley, and lemon juice. Pour over the fillets and serve immediately.

Chapter Four

THE CITY GROWS: SIDE DISHES AND VEGETABLES

Tombstone often had fresh vegetables, either from local gardens or nearby warm climates like California. Side dishes and vegetables were given their own section on bills of fare, unless you ordered from the "Entrée" section, where the chef chose your sides to accompany the dish. Diners chose from each category on the menu for the same price.

BOSTON BAKED BEANS ✇

The mercantile firm of Tasker, Pridham and Company became Pridham, Macneil and Moore after Joseph Tasker left the business in 1883. Their ads claimed they were "the family grocery store" and would supply boardinghouses, restaurants, and families at "bed-rock" prices. They advertised the best and cheapest of the day when the merchants shopped for Los Gatos flour, sugar-cured hams, or Budweiser beer. This recipe was adapted from *One Thousand and One Useful Recipes and Valuable Hints About Cooking and Housekeeping*.

SERVES 4–6

4 cups dried or 1 (32-ounce) can navy beans

Boiling water

1 teaspoon baking soda

½ pound salt pork or bacon

1 tablespoon salt

2 tablespoons molasses

3 tablespoons brown sugar

1 cup tomato sauce

½ teaspoon mustard

Cover the beans with water and allow to soak overnight. Drain the beans and add enough cold water to cover them again. Add the baking soda. Simmer until the bean skins burst, about 30 minutes. (Skip these steps if using canned beans.)

Drain and place beans in a deep baking dish.

Score the rind of the salt pork and add to the dish with the beans. Be sure to leave the rind exposed when placing the pork in the beans. (If using bacon, cut into ¼-inch pieces.)

Combine the remaining ingredients in a bowl and blend well. Pour over beans, making sure the mixture covers the beans completely. If it doesn't, add a little boiling water and stir well. Place a cover or aluminum foil over the beans and bake at 300°F for 1–2 hours, or until beans are soft. Uncover beans during the last 20 minutes of cooking.

CRANBERRY SAUCE ℘

Tombstone churches often sold meals and baked goods to raise funds for various causes. One year, the Methodist church offered traditional Thanksgiving fare. The ladies set the tables at six o'clock, and they were loaded with turkey, urns of cranberry sauce, mince and pumpkin pies, frosted cakes, jellies, jams, fruits, and steaming kettles of coffee and tea. This recipe was adapted from Yuma's *Arizona Sentinel*, November 14, 1885.

SERVES 4–6

2 cups water

4 cups fresh cranberries

Peel of 2 oranges

2 cups sugar

Juice of ½ orange

Bring the water, cranberries, and orange peel to a boil in a large pot. Continue to boil until the skins of the berries have burst, and then add the sugar and orange juice, and reduce the heat to simmer for 5–10 minutes. Chill before serving.

BAKED MACARONI AND CHEESE ✧

Today this dish is an American comfort food, but it originated in France and was brought to the United States by Thomas Jefferson. Early macaroni didn't look like our modern elbow macaroni noodles. They were longer and looked like today's ziti pasta. Recipes back in the day suggested breaking the macaroni into pieces before cooking. This dish appeared on many Tombstone bills of fare and is adapted from *Mrs. Beeton's Dictionary of Every-day Cookery*.

SERVES 4–6

4 cups elbow macaroni, cooked

1 cup grated cheddar cheese

⅓ cup butter, cut into pieces

½ teaspoon salt

Pepper to taste

½ cup cream

¼ cup grated Parmesan cheese

In a buttered baking dish, layer the macaroni, cheddar cheese, and butter. Sprinkle with salt and pepper; add the cream. Cover and bake at 350°F for 25 minutes. Add the Parmesan cheese and broil until the cheese melts. Allow to sit for 10 minutes; stir and serve.

MACARONI À LA ITALIENNE WITH TOMATO SAUCE ⁓

Tombstone's residents had no shortage of places to eat in 1882. There were about seventeen, including the Melrose at 426 Fremont Street, although it was now owned by Maine natives Jane Harding and Catherine Lang. The Russ House continued to prosper, as did the restaurants of Julius Caesar, Walsh and Shanahan, and Robert Campbell. A few of the newer restaurants, or those that had rebuilt, included Pauline Jones's International Restaurant, Charles Langpaap's bakery, McCullough and Tripp's Pacific Chop House, Gregory's Restaurant, and George Modini's on Allen, near 6th. Some of these featured European cuisine like German and Italian dishes, but these dishes only played a small role on their menus. This recipe was adapted from Tucson's *Arizona Weekly Enterprise*, November 18, 1882.

SERVES 2–4

¾ cup macaroni noodle of your choice, uncooked

½ onion

2 teaspoons butter

1½ cups Tomato Sauce (see next page)

½ cup grated Parmesan cheese

1 tablespoon red wine

Place the macaroni, onion, and butter in a medium pot of boiling water. Cook until the macaroni is barely tender, about 15 minutes. Drain and return the macaroni to the pot. Add the tomato sauce, cheese, and wine; heat through and serve.

TOMATO SAUCE ✍

MAKES 1½ CUPS

1¾ cups crushed tomatoes

¼ cup chopped onion

2 teaspoons butter

2 tablespoons flour

¼ teaspoon salt

½ teaspoon freshly
ground pepper

½ teaspoon oregano

½ teaspoon chopped
fresh parsley

In a large skillet, cook the tomatoes and onion over medium heat until onions are lightly browned. Strain and set aside. Add the butter and flour to the skillet and cook over medium heat for 2–3 minutes. Gradually stir in the tomatoes, onion, and oregano; cook until slightly thickened. Add the salt, pepper, and parsley before serving.

TOMBSTONE'S ARSONIST

Not all of Tombstone's businesses were successful, and many business owners just packed up and left for greener pastures. That was not the case with longtime merchant M. Calisher and Company. When they fell on hard times, they were forced to assign their stock back to the company's creditors. By early March 1882, the creditors had almost completely sold the assignment through private sales.

On the night of March 5, David Calisher, in a desperate attempt to salvage something, did the unthinkable in a dusty, dry town. He attempted to set fire to his building, intending to collect the insurance money. The store was insured for $1,800 and the adjoining shoe store for $800. Calisher left kerosene-soaked papers in an oilcan sitting under some wooden shelves. Fortunately for Tombstone, policemen James Kinney and Joseph Poynton noticed the flames and sounded the fire alarm. The hook-and-ladder team arrived on the scene, tore down the burning shelves, and extinguished the flames with buckets of water because the hydrants had been temporarily turned off. Calisher would have known about this because the shut-off notice had been published in the paper the previous day. Although Calisher failed at his attempt, the preceding year's June fire remained fresh in townspeople's minds. When they realized what he had done, they cried, "Lynch him! Hang him!" The feeling was so strong that Calisher sought police protection. The police promptly arrested him and offered refuge in the county jail. His bail was set at $1,500.

The following month, Bisbee merchant E. T. Hardy announced that he had taken over Calisher's old store. The *Epitaph* reported that Hardy was "another live businessman, one who has confidence in the town and acts on his convictions."

LIMA BEANS ✦

Restaurants and lodgings boomed in 1882, and Mrs. S. J. Dill opened her American Restaurant on Allen Street. Mrs. M. L. Woods, who had previously owned the Melrose Restaurant, opened a boardinghouse at 617 Fremont. She charged $8 per week for room and board and served 50-cent meals. By 1884 it was called the Melrose Lodging House. Ed Terroll and Company opened a French restaurant at 510 Allen that was next door to Cadwell and Stanford's grocery, which sold produce like lima beans. This recipe was adapted from San Francisco's *Daily Bulletin Supplement*, October 13, 1883.

SERVES 4

---

4 cups water

1 teaspoon salt

4 cups fresh lima beans

1 tablespoon butter

¼ teaspoon freshly ground pepper

Cream, optional

Boil the water in a medium stockpot; add the salt and lima beans. Reduce the heat to medium and cook covered for 25–30 minutes, or until the beans become tender. Drain and toss with butter, pepper, and additional salt, if desired. Add enough cream to make a light gravy.

CABBAGE ✌

In the spring of 1882, John L. McCullough opened his New York Coffee Saloon and Restaurant at 203 4th Street. His well-cooked and neatly served items included breads, pies, and coffee with cake for 15 cents. Around this time, Robert and Bridget Campbell returned from San Francisco and established a new eatery called the St. Louis Restaurant. When they left in 1881, their New Orleans Restaurant became the property of T. A. and Pauline Jones, who relocated to the corner of 1st and Toughnut Streets. A couple months later, the Campbells moved their new St. Louis Restaurant to their old restaurant location, where they served a variety of meals like this recipe, adapted from Prescott's *Weekly Arizona Miner*, October 7, 1871.

SERVES 4–6

1 head cabbage

½ teaspoon salt

3 teaspoons butter

Salt and pepper to taste

Dill weed to garnish

Wash the cabbage and remove the outside leaves. Cut into quarters and remove the white center stalk.

Place the cabbage and salt in a large stockpot and cover with cold water. Bring to a boil over high heat and cook uncovered for 40–50 minutes, or until cabbage has reached the desired tenderness. Drain the cabbage and return it to the stockpot. Add the butter and salt and pepper to taste. Garnish with dill weed.

ASPARAGUS ✣

In May 1882, well-known Tombstone caterer "Jakey" Jacobs reopened the Grand, which was housed in the new front addition at 422 Allen Street. Originally designed as a store, it was spacious, with high ceilings that made it feel bright and airy. It contained six elegant private dining rooms, a public dining hall with four tables, and a family dining hall. The *Epitaph* wrote, "The fact that Jacobs has taken the dining room to the Grand is an assurance to the public that Tombstone is fast to have an eating house worthy of the town. 'Jakey' is the boss caterer of Arizona, 'don't you forget it.'" He created a window display that sported a fountain filled with rocks, plants, and fish. Window borders of plants also surrounded the centerpiece of wild game, fish, and choice cuts of meat to tempt walkers-by. He had competition from druggist Clement Eschman & Co., who ran the Grotto beneath the Grand and advertised that imported lunches and fine beer were their specialty. This was especially convenient for the miners below-ground, who had easy access to the Grotto. It would later become the Fountain Saloon, where Alderson and John Grattan served more than thirty different lunch specialties, including pâté de foie gras. While Jacobs was wildly successful, he left the Grand at the end of 1882. It was then taken over by William Goldbaum and J. M. Owen. This recipe was adapted from San Francisco's *Daily Examiner*, August 12, 1874.

SERVES 2

1 pound asparagus

1 tablespoon butter

½ teaspoon salt

¼ teaspoon freshly ground pepper

Remove bottoms of the asparagus by either cutting with a knife or snapping with your hands. The ends should snap off where the tender part ends and the tough part begins. Place the spears in a large pot of boiling, salted water. Cook for 15 minutes, or until tender. Drain and toss with butter and salt and pepper.

TOMBSTONE'S 1882 FIRES

On May 25, 1882, a second great fire destroyed four blocks in Tombstone's business district. This time the damage was west of 5th Street—the side the 1881 fire had spared. The fire showed no mercy, not caring what it consumed as long as it was being fed. The fire quickly devastated most of Tombstone's largest hotels and restaurants, including Brown's, Bayley's Restaurant, the Cosmopolitan Hotel, the Maison Doree, and the Grand Hotel. Also lost to the fire were the Rockaway Oyster House and Fitzhenry and Mansfield's. Thomas Ward's City Meat Market, which he had recently moved to 511 Allen, was also destroyed. The Occidental Chop House succumbed to the fire as well.

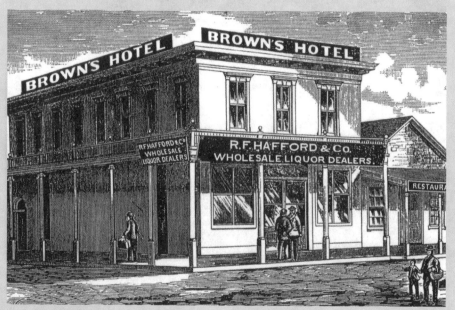

Artist's rendition of Brown's Hotel in 1880 after the second-story addition was completed
ARIZONA QUARTERLY ILLUSTRATED, 1880

None of the existing hotels were rebuilt. Jacob Everhardy's Fremont Street Market was destroyed, but he rebuilt. Julius and Sophie Caesar lost their bakery and restaurant but had reopened by July, once again serving tasty dishes to residents. The fire fiend also destroyed the Campbells' recently opened restaurant, but even without insurance, they reopened.

Lodging became a concern for anyone visiting Tombstone. To fill this void, several new lodging houses emerged. One of note was the newly built Palace Lodging House run by Lucy Young, who once owned the Star Restaurant. The Palace was said to be the most attractive in town. The two-story building, located on 5th Street between Allen and Toughnut, had twenty-five well-ventilated guest rooms, each with a view; it even had a bathroom on the second floor. It was taken over by Mrs. Immel two years later. Another boardinghouse opened when William and Isabella "Belle" LeVan opened the LeVan House at 533–535 Allen, across from the Wells-Fargo office. The newlywed couple offered furnished and unfurnished rooms on the second floor over Charles Langpaap's restaurant and Samuel McLaren's saloon.

Just as Tombstone's business district recovered from its second devastating fire, another blazed in late July. This third fire was not as ferocious as its predecessors, largely because of the town's new waterworks. This fire started in a back bedroom of German native Pauline Jones's New Orleans Restaurant, at the corner of 1st and Toughnut Streets. Since the restaurant was constructed of wood, there was not much hope of saving it or the building next to it. Fortunately for Tombstone, the New Orleans Restaurant was around the corner from the Rescue Hook and Ladder Company, which was able to use the newly installed water system to suppress the flames.

SUGAR PEAS

After the 1882 fire, Tombstone had about six places to stay in town, including the LeVan Lodging House, Charles Brickwedel's Way Up Lodging House, and the Aztec House. Some of the grocers included Cadwell and Stanford's, Frank Austin, Gates and Hickey's, Milich and Dyar's, and Fitzhenry and Mansfield's. John Fitzhenry took a break from the business world to marry Blanche Shakelford of Los Angeles, but the couple returned to Tombstone so that John could get back to selling goods and produce to Tombstone's residents and businesses. This recipe was adapted from *One Thousand and One Useful Recipes and Valuable Hints About Cooking and Housekeeping.*

SERVES 2–4

7–8 quarts water

4 teaspoons salt

3 cups shelled tender sweet peas

Salt and pepper to taste

1½ teaspoons sugar

6 tablespoons butter, cut into pieces

Bring the water and salt to a boil in a large pot. Add the peas and allow the water to return to a boil. Boil gently, uncovered, for 7 minutes. Test the peas for firmness. If you like your peas more tender, continue boiling, checking frequently.

Drain immediately. Place the peas back in the pot; add the salt, pepper, and sugar. Roll the peas around in the pan to coat evenly. Put peas in a serving bowl and dot the top with butter.

TURNIPS ✺

Even though dining out was a popular pastime in Tombstone, many enjoyed eating at the Methodist church's occasional fund-raising events. At one event they prepared an old-fashioned New England–style lunch that offered the rich flavor of home cooking. The food was served at the Miner's Exchange between eleven and two o'clock. Turnips were a popular vegetable used to make New England boiled dinners. This recipe was adapted from San Francisco's *Daily Examiner*, August 12, 1874.

SERVES 2

---

3 medium turnips

½ teaspoon salt

4 tablespoons butter

Salt and pepper to taste

Parsley sprigs to garnish

Peel the turnips and cut into cubes. Place the cubed turnips and salt in a medium pot and cover with cold water. Bring to a boil and continue cooking for about 25 minutes, or until tender. Drain the turnips and mash them. Add the butter and salt and pepper to taste. Garnish with parsley sprigs.

Note: If you can't get turnips, try substituting rutabagas. They're delicious too.

STRING BEANS ✌

In December 1882, George Pridham, of Tasker and Pridham's, sold half his mercantile store to Donald A. Macneil. The firm was still known as Tasker and Pridham's, although Macneil now owned 25 percent. Macneil was also part owner of a wholesale grocery store in town with L. W. Carr and H. E. Hills, a former merchant who had closed his own business a year ago. Joe Hoefler was another businessman who reopened his store, and by the end of the year had another on the corner of 5th and Fremont Streets. These merchants continued to keep Tombstone fed with their many supplies, like fresh green beans. This recipe was adapted from *The Physiology of Taste: Harder's Book of Practical American Cookery.*

SERVES 4–6

2 pounds green string beans

5 quarts water

1 teaspoon chopped shallots

3 tablespoons butter

¼ teaspoon salt

⅛ teaspoon freshly ground pepper

Juice from ½ lemon

Boil the beans in the water for 10–15 minutes, or until tender. Drain the beans and run under cold water to stop the cooking process. Drain again. Sauté the cooked beans and shallots in the butter over medium-high heat, stirring often to coat with butter. Season with salt, pepper, and lemon juice.

NEW POTATOES ❧

The Occidental Chop House continued to serve its usual fare, which included steak and potatoes. The *Epitaph* printed a funny story on that subject:

"A boarder at the Occidental gazed upon his plate one morning and said, 'Is there a reliable physician stopping in this house?'

'Yes, sir,' said the waiter.

'Good surgeon, too, eh?'

'Believe so, sir.'

'Then you just see if he is in his room before I start on breakfast. I had a brother choked to death on a steak like that once, and I'm bound to take all the necessary precautions.'"

This recipe was adapted from San Francisco's *Daily Examiner*, February 5, 1879.

SERVES 2–4

10–12 small new potatoes

¼ cup butter

½ teaspoon salt

¼ teaspoon freshly ground pepper

1 tablespoon chopped fresh parsley

Boil the potatoes in salted water for 15 minutes, or until tender. Remove and drain. Melt the butter in a large skillet over medium heat and add the potatoes. Sprinkle with the salt, pepper, and parsley. Cook long enough for the potatoes to be coated evenly with the seasonings.

MASHED POTATOES ❧

Nellie Cashman, along with her sister Frances "Fannie" Cunningham, opened a new hotel in 1881 where they served meals that included potatoes. It was called the American at 427 and 429 Fremont Street and contained a large dining hall where elegant meals were served at all hours. Nellie and Fannie operated their business successfully until 1882. This recipe was adapted from *One Thousand and One Useful Recipes and Valuable Hints About Cooking and Housekeeping*.

SERVES 2–4

5 large potatoes, peeled and sliced

½ teaspoon salt

3 tablespoons butter

¼ teaspoon freshly ground pepper

⅓–½ cup milk or cream

Place the potatoes and salt in a large pot of cold water; bring to a boil. Cook over high heat for 15–20 minutes, or until just tender. Immediately drain the potatoes and mash them. Add the butter, pepper, and additional salt if desired. Gradually add enough milk or cream to reach a fluffy consistency.

Note: For a special treat, try adding ½ cup grated Parmesan or Romano cheese.

FRENCH BAKED POTATOES ✺

Russ House owner Joseph Pascholy visited California for two weeks in 1882 and arranged for the Russ House to receive weekly shipments of fresh fish, fruits, and vegetables to ensure his patrons had the best. This recipe was adapted from the 1885 journal of Arizona resident Martha Summerhayes, found in an Arizona Historical Society collection.

SERVES 6–8

6 large peeled potatoes

4 tablespoons butter

1 onion, sliced

1 cup milk

Salt and pepper to taste

A few gratings of nutmeg

1 double piecrust (see recipe on page 154)

Boil and rice the potatoes (if you don't have a ricer, just mash them). While the potatoes are cooking, sauté the onion in 1 tablespoon butter until golden. Add the onions, remaining butter, milk, salt, pepper, and nutmeg to potatoes; mix well.

Line a pie pan with one of the crusts. Fill it with the potato mixture and put on the top crust. Bake in a 350°F oven for about 30 minutes, or until the crust is golden.

Note: While the original recipe uses a piecrust, this can be made without it. If skipping the piecrust, just butter the pan and bake until the top is golden.

SWEET POTATOES ✑

Aristotle Petro of the Occidental Chop House left Tombstone in the spring of 1882 and sold his restaurant to Peter Claudianos, who moved it to 5th Street. He also hired chef Alvan Young, who had previously worked at the chophouse. Although he was fortunate to find a good cook, Claudianos was not so lucky when it came to the restaurant's supplies. In April a "dead broke" stole two turkeys from the chophouse. Claudianos reported the theft to the police, and his turkeys, which had already been sold to "Jakey" Jacobs, who was now with the Pacific Chop House, were returned promptly by Jacobs. The unknown thief got away with Jacobs's $6. Alvan Young continued to serve tasty dishes like these sweet potatoes at the Occidental. This recipe was adapted from Bellevue, Louisiana's, *Bossier Banner*, November 20, 1879.

SERVES 4–6

6 sweet potatoes

6 tablespoons butter

Cinnamon and sugar, optional

Wash the potatoes and pat dry. Bake on a foil-lined baking sheet at 375°F for 40–45 minutes, or until tender. Slice the potatoes lengthwise and butter them. Add cinnamon and sugar if desired for additional sweetness.

EUREKA RESTAURANT CON

The Eureka Restaurant on Toughnut Street also disappeared rather quickly, but fire was not the reason for its demise. Mrs. Inez McMartin opened her restaurant in June 1881 and hired James Lane to manage it. Lane had been in Tombstone for about five months and was reportedly the best restaurant man on the Pacific coast. Even though McMartin hired the best manager and her bills of fare featured bountiful and inexpensive meals, her restaurant closed in September.

McMartin was a shrewd businesswoman, and even more shrewd when it came to deceit. After McMartin opened her business, she mortgaged it twice to two unsuspecting mortgagors: Miss Emma Parker and J. S. McCoy. McCoy managed the Huachuca Water Company, and Parker was a woman of somewhat questionable character. Neither knew that the other had already mortgaged McMartin's property. McMartin was also indebted to a local butcher for $80. McMartin and her paramour, Joseph Price, a 31-year-old steward, skipped town, but Cochise County's Sheriff Johnny Behan saw the two in Benson. At the time, Behan was unaware of the recent dupe they had committed. Upon returning to Tombstone, Behan was advised of the crime, and authorities in Deming, New Mexico, El Paso, Texas, and Denver, Colorado, were notified in an effort to capture the criminals. Unfortunately, the damage was done. Parker was out $300, and McCoy had an uncollectable debt of $200. To top things off, McMartin had sold her mortgaged property before she left, leaving her creditors no way to collect.

Tombstone ended 1882 with prosperous and sophisticated living that included successful businesses, productive mines, and even limited telephone service. Tombstone's most impressive new building was its courthouse, and it was nearly complete. When finished it stood two stories high, was constructed of brick, and cost $43,000. It sat one block over from the main street of Allen Street, where many hotels and restaurants served tasty dishes.

The Eureka Restaurant,
On Toughnut St., near Vizina Works.

Mrs. McMartin, Proprietress,
James Lane, Manager,
[The oldest hotel man on the coast.]

BILL OF FARE.

SOUPS.
Chicken.   Rice.   Tomato.   Mullagatany.
FISH.
Fresh Fish. Egg Sauce.
ROASTS.
Beef. Mutton.   Leg of Mutton, Caper Sauce,
Stuffed Veal.   Lamb and Green Peas.
Chicken and Duck.
ENTREES.
Chicken Fricassee.   Stewed Kidney.   Giblets,
Stewed Beef, German Style.   Beef a la mode.
VEGETABLES.
Mashed and Baked Potatoes.   Green Corn. String
Beans.   Stewed Tomatoes.
PANTRY.
Peach and Apple Pies. Indian and Sago Pudding.
DESSERT.
Prunes.   Oranges and Nuts.   Jll tf

Despite their dubious morality, McMartin and Lane offered their patrons a bountiful menu in June 1881.

THE *TOMBSTONE EPITAPH*, JUNE 11, 1882

Chapter Five

THE PINNACLE: SAUCES AND CONDIMENTS

Sauces and condiments were not readily available like they are today, but some were sold in bottles and jars in the 1800s. Did you know that some of the products we use today were created in the 1800s? Items included Heinz sweet mixed pickles, Lea & Perrins Worcestershire Sauce, and bottled catsup from Crosse & Blackwell of London. The well-known Underwood Deviled Ham was born then, as was Coleman's Mustard. Despite these ready-made products, many chefs and cooks prided themselves on making their own.

HOMEMADE MAYONNAISE ❧

Some of Tombstone's restaurants experienced change in 1885. The Star Restaurant, owned by Mrs. Annie B. Paddock-Coyle, was taken over by Mrs. Bockman. The New York Restaurant, Bakery and Coffee House closed when owners Julius and Sophie Caesar purchased a half interest in the Crystal Palace Saloon. Bernhardt "Ben" Wehrfritz had been the sole owner of the Crystal Palace since his former partner, Siegfried Tribolet, left to start his own brewery. When their partnership dissolved in 1882, Tribolet took the Golden Eagle name with him. Wehrfritz's brewery became the Crystal Palace. The Crystal Palace Saloon had a separate entrance to Fred Parker's Crystal Palace Lunch Parlors on 5th Street. His offerings included sandwiches, hot lunches, and oysters served in all styles. Meals at the lunch parlors cost 2 bits and up. Try this recipe, adapted from the 1872 *California Recipe Book*, to make your next sandwich.

MAKES 2 CUPS

1 hard-boiled egg yolk

1 raw egg yolk

½ teaspoon salt

Dash of cayenne pepper

2 teaspoons apple cider vinegar

½ teaspoon yellow mustard

1½ teaspoons lemon juice

2 cups oil

Combine the eggs in a bowl and whip well. Add the salt, pepper, vinegar, mustard, and lemon juice. Slowly add the oil, drop by drop, while whipping the entire time. Do this until the oil is gone and you have a smooth, creamy mayonnaise.

Note: You can substitute premade mayonnaise, but add the mustard and then taste the salad for seasoning. Adjust with salt and cayenne pepper.

KETCHUP (TOMATO CATSUP) ✥

Frank Wolcott was the manager of Woodhead and Gay's Cash Store in 1883, and when Seth Owens of the Grand Hotel sold his business, Wolcott paid $1,200 for the restaurant's chairs, tables, curtains, mirrors, table linens, chandeliers, and everything else that could be removed. This purchase allowed him to open his own grocery and provision store on 5th, between Allen and Fremont Streets, that lasted until after the turn of the century. His business location doubled as his residence, as was the case for many of Tombstone's businesspeople. After Frank opened his store, he hired Thomas Allison as salesman and DeWitt Messick, who later became Wolcott's business partner. Items like bottled ketchup were sold, but many people made their own. The original recipe, adapted from San Francisco's *Daily Bulletin Supplement*, September 23, 1876, noted that the recipe would keep for twenty years if corked properly!

MAKES 2 CUPS

2½ cups tomatoes

1 teaspoon salt

½ teaspoon whole peppercorns, bruised

3 teaspoons red pepper flakes

½ teaspoon cinnamon sticks

¼ teaspoon freshly grated nutmeg

¾ teaspoon mustard seed

½ teaspoon whole allspice

3 garlic cloves, peeled and sliced

¼ teaspoon whiskey, brandy, or cider vinegar

Either cook fresh tomatoes to yield 2½ cups or use canned. Place the tomatoes and salt in a saucepan and blend with an immersion blender (or use a blender before placing in the saucepan). Put the remainder of the spices in a piece of cheesecloth and tie. If using vinegar, add it now.

Bring tomatoes and salt to a boil; add the spice bag. Cook over low heat for about 1–3 hours, until ketchup reaches your desired thickness. Remove from the heat and take out the spice bag. If using whiskey or brandy, add it now. Put ketchup in a storage container and refrigerate.

CHOW CHOW ✌

This recipe, adapted from California's *Sacramento Daily Record-Union*, September 3, 1886, is a good way to use up all the leftovers from the garden at the end of the season and preserve the harvest for winter use.

MAKES ABOUT 6 PINTS

1 large cauliflower

12 small cucumbers

6 celery stalks

12 small onions

3 red peppers

2 cups fresh green beans

4 carrots, cut into strips

¼ cup salt

1 gallon white vinegar

6 tablespoons mustard seed

1 teaspoon freshly ground pepper

1 teaspoon whole cloves

1 cinnamon stick

2 teaspoons turmeric

Cut all the vegetables except carrots into small pieces; place in a large bowl. Sprinkle with salt and let stand for 24 hours. Drain off any excess liquid. In a large stockpot, bring the vinegar and spices to a boil. Add the vegetables and continue cooking until slightly tender.

Pack into hot pint jars, being sure to leave a ½-inch headspace in the jars. Tighten the lids and set in boiling water that covers the jars. When the water begins to boil again, cook for 15 minutes. Remove from the water and set on counter to cool.

PICCALILLI ✤

Chandler and Forsyth's C.O.D. House at 328 Fremont Street opened in 1882 and immediately placed a large ad in the *Commercial Advertiser*, noting that they sold cheese, bananas, oatmeal, eggs, butter, tapioca, macaroni, crackers, potatoes, and onions. Their mottos were "Cash Talks" and "Cheap for Cash." The editor of the paper remarked, "By paying cash you will save ten percent, which is quite an item." J. G. Brown also quietly opened a family grocery store where H. E. Hills's grocery store had been on 4th Street. Woodhead and Gay's store prospered, and they relocated to a larger store on 5th near Fremont. Bottled items like pickles and relishes were often sold at these stores, but they were also popular to make at home. This recipe was adapted from the *Arizona Sentinel*, November 12, 1887.

MAKES 6 PINTS

2 cups diced green tomatoes

¼ cup chopped horseradish

2 green peppers, diced

1 onion, diced

1 small head cabbage, diced

½ cup chopped celery

½ cup salt

1½ cups vinegar

½ teaspoon ground mustard seed

4 cloves

½ teaspoon ground cinnamon

Place the chopped vegetables in a large stockpot and sprinkle with salt. Let stand overnight. Drain off any liquid; add the vinegar and remaining ingredients. Cook over medium heat until slightly tender, stirring occasionally.

Fill clean pint jars, leaving a ½-inch headspace, and seal. Place the pints in boiling water to cover. When the water returns to a boil, cook for 15 minutes. Remove and allow to cool.

Chapter Six
THE FINALE:
DESSERTS

It's hard to imagine that anyone would have room for dessert after looking at the lengthy bills of fare from Tombstone's restaurants. Clearly, many did, as evidenced by the variety of options, including pies, cakes, ice cream, puddings, and other yummy treats.

RUSS HOUSE.

Sunday Bill of Fare—Oct. 30 at 4:30 p. m. Toughnut Time.

SOUPS.
Chicken and Consomme.

FISH.
Brook Trout, Frois a l'Huile.

BOILED.
Lamb, Caper Sauce,
Beef a l'.Espanol,
Corned Beef.

ESTREES.
Breast of Lamb breaded a la Mayonnaise,
Croquettes of Rice, Kirchwasser Sauce,
Chicken Fricasco, a la Creme,
Salim of Chicken. Giblets,
Calf' Head, en Tortue.

ROASTS.
Prime Beef, Ribs of Beef,
Leg of Mutton, Stuffed Lamb,
Dressed Veal, Pork, Apple Sauce,
and Chicken.

VEGETABLES.
Sugar Peas, Tomatoes,
Corn, Turnips and
Mashed Potatoes.

PASTRY.
Assorted Pies and Jelly Roll.

PUDDING
New York Plum, Heart Sauce, Lemon
Flavor.

DESERT.
Grapes and Walnuts.

SALADS.
Lobster, Tomatoes, Beets
and Horse Radish.

RELISHES.
Assorted.

The October 30, 1881, bill of fare for the Russ House
TOMBSTONE DAILY NUGGET,
OCTOBER 30, 1881

JELLY CAKE

The Russ House remained a very popular hotel, and to ensure their guests were well taken care of, Nellie Cashman and her sister Frances Cunningham employed Sol Anderson to mix the cocktails, Alex Bacilli to stock the pantry, and Charles Blair to wait on guests. With her staff set and her sister to take charge, Nellie and a party of hopeful miners headed to the gold fields in lower California. She ditched her proper Victorian dress and laced boots and wore a conventional male miner's outfit that included black pants, a blue shirt, and high-top American boots. Upon her return in June 1883, she told the *Arizona Weekly Citizen*, "I think that I have returned with the major portion of the fortunes to be obtained in Lower California, which consist of cacti, rocks and Spanish bayonet." She promptly went back to the Russ House, where she served up delicious meals and cakes like this one, whose recipe was adapted from the 1872 *California Recipe Book*.

SERVES 6–8

2 cups flour

1 teaspoon cream of tartar

½ teaspoon baking soda

Nutmeg to taste

1 cup sugar

½ cup butter, room temperature

3 eggs, room temperature

½ cup milk

Jelly for spreading

Preheat oven to 350°F. Combine flour, cream of tartar, baking soda, and nutmeg in a small bowl.

Cream sugar and butter together in a large bowl until light and fluffy. Add eggs, one a time, beating after each addition.

Starting and ending with the flour, alternately add flour and milk to creamed mixture; beat well until incorporated.

Line and grease two 8-inch cake pans; divide the batter between them.

Bake for 20–30 minutes, or until done. Cool in pans for 5 minutes; remove to cake racks and cool completely.

Spread jelly between cake layers and on top. Dust with powdered sugar if desired.

BOSTON CREAM PIE ✎

While the title of this dessert has the word "pie" in its name, this is really a cake. It was originally baked in a pie pan, so that's how it got its name. Even though it was wildly popular all over the West, it was created in Boston at the Omni Parker House in 1856. The original recipe had a chocolate ganache topping. However, this recipe, adapted from California's *Placer Herald*, February 12, 1876, and many other sources, did not call for any topping other than powdered sugar because chocolate was expensive and often hard to come by.

MAKES 1 DOUBLE-LAYER CAKE

7 eggs, separated

1 cup sugar

1 cup flour

2 tablespoons melted butter

Pastry Cream Filling (recipe follows)

Divide the egg yolks and whites into two bowls and add ½ cup of the sugar to each. Beat the egg yolks until light yellow and the whites until medium peaks form. Using a whisk, fold the whites into the yolks; stir to blend. Gradually add the flour and blend. Add the butter and blend again.

Pour mixture into a greased 10-inch cake pan. Bake at 350°F for about 20 minutes, or until spongy and golden. Test with a toothpick; if it comes out clean, the cake is done. Cool cake in the pan for 10 minutes. Remove cake from the pan and set on a cake rack.

When completely cooled, cut the cake in half horizontally, so you have a top and bottom. Spread pastry cream filling over one layer and top with the second. Dust with powdered sugar.

PASTRY CREAM FILLING ✺

MAKES 2 CUPS

1 cup cream

1 cup milk

½ cup sugar

¼ cup flour

¼ teaspoon salt

4 eggs, beaten

1 tablespoon butter

1 teaspoon vanilla
or dark rum

Scald the cream and milk in a large saucepan (until bubbles appear around the edge). Meanwhile, combine the sugar, flour, and salt in a small bowl.

Add flour mixture to the scalded liquid. Cook over medium heat, stirring constantly, until mixture has thickened, about 5 minutes.

In a small bowl, slowly add ½ cup of the cooked mixture to the beaten eggs, stirring constantly. Add the eggs to the saucepan and stir continuously for 2 minutes.

Add the butter and vanilla or rum; mix well. Remove from the heat and cool.

MARBLE CAKE WITH CHOCOLATE FUDGE ICING ✑

Robert and Bridget Campbell owned the St. Louis Restaurant but were able to change back to its original name—New Orleans—in June 1882. They also announced that they were back at their old location on 4th Street. Six months later Bridget suddenly became ill with violent spasms and stomach cramps. She was prescribed medicine, but the pain did not subside. Another doctor was called. He gave her a morphine injection, and she died a few minutes later, on December 1. The *Epitaph* called for an investigation, and the coroner ruled that she died of natural causes.

The Rockaway Oyster House had been rebuilt and was now called the Rockaway Restaurant. It was still operated under the skillful ownership of John Bogovich and Company and even offered a private dining room for female patrons to enjoy items like this cake recipe, adapted from *One Thousand and One Useful Recipes and Valuable Hints About Cooking and Housekeeping.*

MAKES 1 CAKE

⅔ cup butter, room temperature

1¾ cups sugar

4 eggs, beaten

1 teaspoon vanilla

3⅓ cups cake flour

4 teaspoons baking powder

1 teaspoon salt

1 cup milk

2 ounces (1 square) chocolate, melted

Chocolate Fudge Icing (recipe follows)

In a large bowl, cream the butter and sugar together until well combined. Add eggs and vanilla. Mix well.

In a separate bowl, sift the dry ingredients together.

Gradually add the dry ingredients to the egg mixture, alternating with the milk. Beat until smooth. Pour one-third of the batter into a separate bowl and add the melted chocolate. Stir to combine.

Grease and flour a 10-inch tube pan. Drop the batter into the pan by spoonfuls, alternating the vanilla and chocolate batters.

Bake at 350°F for 1 hour, or until done. Test for doneness by inserting a toothpick into the cake; if it comes out clean, the cake is done. Allow the cake to cool in the pan for 15 minutes. Turn onto a cake rack and cool completely before frosting.

CHOCOLATE FUDGE ICING ⤸

MAKES ABOUT 2 CUPS

¼ cup milk

2 ounces baking chocolate

3 tablespoons butter

3 cups powdered sugar

1 teaspoon vanilla

In a large saucepan, combine the first three ingredients. Cook over low heat until the chocolate has melted. Stir in the sugar and vanilla and cook over medium heat for 3–5 minutes, until the mixture bubbles.

Remove from the heat, strain, and immediately pour over the cake. Allow to harden, and serve.

This bill of fare from when Jennie ran the Boss House included a variety of items for hungry patrons.
THE *TOMBSTONE EPITAPH*, JUNE 11, 1882

BOSS DINNER
AT THE
Boss Restaurant.

Bill of Fare for Sunday Dinner.
SOUP.
Oyster Soup and Chicken Broth.
ROASTS.
Roast Beef. Roast Pork and Apple Sauce. Lamb
and Green Peas. Chicken Roast
and Fricasseed.
VEGETABLES.
Cabbage. Turnips. Green Corn. Tomatoes and
Potatoes.
DESSERT.
English Plum Pudding. Ice Cocoanut Cake.
Jelly Rolls. Marble Cake. Raisin,
Custard and Green Peach Pie.
BEVERAGES.
Tea. Coffee. Claret Wine.
Mrs. Jennie Harding, Proprietress.
Allen Street, between Sixth and Seventh.
Jll lt

COCONUT CAKE ❧

The Occidental Hotel had a first-class restaurant, appropriately named the Occidental. This restaurant was not associated with Aristotle Petro's establishment of the same name, which once served Tombstonians elegant French meals. Petro's restaurant had closed earlier in the year. The new Occidental restaurant was run by Jennie Harden, who once owned the Boss Restaurant at 605 Allen Street. Harden had sold the restaurant to Miss Long, who hired Sallie Fletcher to work for her at the Boss, where they offered this cake. This recipe was adapted from California's *Sacramento Daily Record-Union*, September 24, 1881.

MAKES 1 CAKE

⅔ cup butter

1¾ cups sugar

3 cups flour

3 teaspoons baking powder

¼ teaspoon salt

1 cup milk

4 eggs

1 teaspoon lemon extract

1 cup shredded coconut

Whipped Cream Filling (recipe follows)

Mint leaves for garnish

In a large bowl, cream butter and sugar. Beat until light and fluffy.

In a small bowl, sift the dry ingredients together.

Combine the milk, eggs, and lemon extract. Alternately add this and the flour mixture to the butter and sugar mixture. Beat on high for 2 minutes.

Pour the batter into three greased and floured 9-inch cake pans. Bake at 350°F for 25 minutes. Remove from the oven and allow to cool in the pans for 10 minutes. Turn the cake layers out onto cake racks to cool completely.

Spread some of the coconut and whipped cream between the cake layers. Spread remaining whipped cream on the top and sides; sprinkle with coconut.

Refrigerate cake for a minimum of 20 minutes. Garnish with mint.

WHIPPED CREAM FILLING ❧

MAKES 2 CUPS

....

2 pints heavy cream	Combine all ingredients in a chilled bowl; whip until fluffy.
4 tablespoons sugar	
1 teaspoon vanilla	

POST–1882 FIRE MAISON DOREE

Even though the Cosmopolitan Hotel and its Maison Doree restaurant were destroyed in Tombstone's second fire in 1882, Stephen DeMartini took the name Maison Doree in 1883. He opened his rotisserie on 5th Street between Allen and Fremont, where George Mandich served up Italian dishes including ravioli and sweet desserts.

In 1884 Armand and Amelia Tuquet took over the Maison Doree. Armand was a well-known French chef who once worked at the Palace Hotel in Tucson. He began his new venture by hiring a cook, but in September 1884 Armand announced that he would be cooking again because his customers were not happy. Amelia took over management of the restaurant, and to manage the dining room they relied on his French friend, Dan Leuch, who came down from Tucson and once owned a Maison Doree in that city. Tuquet loved wine and was once asked about his wine usage. He claimed that he "used" two bottles of claret wine daily but did not drink to excess. In 1886 he left the Maison Doree and opened a French restaurant on Fremont Street when the Gregorys sold their business. At some point they took on Ed Hotopp as a business partner, but he retired in September 1890 and left the Tuquets to run the business.

In 1890 Armand Tuquet's Maison Doree Rotisserie advertised that it was the only first-class French restaurant in town. They also noted that there was a special lady's parlor for women diners. They hired a French cook, who took over in May and claimed that his first meal would be "first-class." The Tuquets moved into one of the Can Can Restaurant's old locations at 409 Allen Street after signing a one-year lease with the property's owner, Siegfried Tribolet. Their Maison Doree, sitting opposite the Occidental Hotel, continued to serve French meals and stayed open day and night. The paper noted: "At the Maison Doree today will be served the usual excellent Sunday dinner. Roast chicken, wild game, all kinds of meats cooked to order, coffee, for which this house is justly celebrated, fine dessert and everything comprising an excellent dinner."

The following year, the Tuquets left and the Maison Doree merged with Jakey's Fashion Restaurant. Armand opened the French Rotisserie in Tucson in 1892 and passed away in 1895. A new chef, Monsieur Gamba, from San Francisco, took over at the Maison Doree in February 1892. In 1893 Pauline Jones took over the Maison Doree from Mr. and Mrs. Miller for a while, and by the end of 1894, Julius Caesar had taken it over. Before that, Caesar served German lunches at a lunchroom in the back of the Crystal Palace. His wife, Sophie, died in 1895, but he stayed in the restaurant business and went on to own various restaurants in nearby Bisbee and Benson.

ALMOND CAKE

Probably the finest hotel in town after the destruction of the Cosmopolitan, Brown's, and the Grand was the Occidental Hotel, which Joseph Pascholy and Siegfried Tribolet opened in March 1883 at the corner of 4th and Allen Streets. This new second-story hotel, covering five lots on Allen Street, easily accommodated one hundred guests and had numerous businesses on the first floor. Pain de Genes is the French name for this cake. The recipe was adapted from *One Thousand and One Useful Recipes and Valuable Hints About Cooking and Housekeeping.*

This image appeared on the hotel's letterhead.

COURTESY OF THE ARIZONA HISTORICAL SOCIETY

SERVES 6–8

⅔ cup almond flour

½ cup sugar

¼ cup flour

½ cup butter

2 eggs

1 teaspoon vanilla extract

3 tablespoons dark rum

Powdered sugar for dusting

Fresh berries and mint leaves for garnish

Preheat oven to 350°F.

Combine the almond flour, sugar, and flour. Mix well and set aside.

Cream the remaining sugar and butter in a large bowl. Add the eggs, one at a time, combining well after each addition. Add the vanilla and rum; beat until completely mixed. Add the almond mixture and blend until smooth.

Butter and slightly flour an 8- or 9-inch cake pan. Line the bottom of the pan with parchment or wax paper. Pour the batter in the pan. Please note that the batter will only come up one-quarter of the way on the pan.

Bake for 30 to 35 minutes, or until cake is golden and pulls away from the sides of the pan. Cool completely, and dust the top with powdered sugar. Garnish with fresh berries and mint leaves.

POUND CAKE ✑

Established grocery merchants Fitzhenry and Mansfield advertised that "they lead them all"; "For the sweetest and best hams and bacon go to Fitzhenry & Mansfield's"; and "Our gilt-edge butter cannot be surpassed." Tombstone cooks needed lots of butter to make this recipe, adapted from Yuma's *Arizona Sentinel*, December 26, 1885.

MAKES 1 CAKE

½ cup butter, softened

1 cup sugar

5 eggs

2 tablespoons brandy

2 cups flour

½ teaspoon freshly grated nutmeg

1 teaspoon baking soda

½ cup milk

Preheat oven to 325°F.

Beat the butter until light and fluffy, about 7 minutes. Add the sugar, eggs, and brandy. Beat for another 5 minutes.

Sift the flour, nutmeg, and baking soda into a separate bowl. Alternating with the milk, add the sifted flour to the butter and sugar. Mix on high for 5 minutes. You want this batter to be light and fluffy.

Pour batter into a greased loaf pan. Bake at 325°F for 1 hour, or until done.

Cool in pan for 10 minutes. Remove and allow to cool completely on a wire rack. Slice and serve with ice cream or fresh fruit.

STRAWBERRY SHORTCAKE ❧

Strawberry shortcake is always a successful dessert, as the ladies of Tombstone's Methodist church could have attested to. This version was adapted from *One Thousand and One Useful Recipes and Valuable Hints About Cooking and Housekeeping.*

MAKES 1 CAKE OR 6–8 INDIVIDUAL SERVINGS

5½ cups strawberries

¼ cup sugar

½ teaspoon salt

3 tablespoons sugar

2 cups flour

1 tablespoon baking powder

½ cup butter

1 egg, beaten

⅔ cup milk

Whipped Cream Filling (see recipe on page 130)

Preheat oven to 450°F.

Place strawberries in a bowl and sprinkle with ¼ cup sugar; set aside.

Mix the dry ingredients in a large bowl with a whisk. Add the butter and cut in with a pastry cutter until crumbly.

In a small bowl, mix the egg and milk together. Pour over the crumbled mixture; stir just enough to moisten.

Spread mixture in a greased 8-inch cake pan and bake at 450°F for 15 minutes. Allow the cake to cool in the pan for 10 minutes; remove. When cool enough to handle, cut the cake in half horizontally. Spread a layer of the whipped cream on the bottom half, then a layer of the strawberries. Top with the upper half and frost with the remaining whipped cream and strawberries. Serve warm.

Note: You can also make individual servings.

LEMON CAKE ✒

Fred Parker outgrew his Crystal Palace lunch parlor and in 1886 moved to Allen Street near 5th. His Elite Restaurant advertised in 1887: "The table is constantly supplied with the very best the market affords. Polite and attentive waiters will attend to your orders. Meals cooked to order at all hours of the day and night." Try this delicious dessert, adapted from the 1872 *California Recipe Book*.

MAKES 1 CAKE

¾ cup butter

1½ cups sugar

3 eggs

Grated peel of 1 lemon

3 cups sifted flour

4 teaspoons baking powder

½ teaspoon salt

½ cup milk

½ cup lemon juice

¼ cup orange juice

Whipped Cream Filling (see recipe on page 130)

Preheat oven to 350°F.

Cream the butter and sugar in a large bowl, beating until light and fluffy. Add eggs one at a time, mixing thoroughly after each addition. Stir in the lemon peel and mix well.

Sift the flour, baking powder, and salt into a small bowl two times. Alternating with the juices and milk, add the flour to the butter and sugar. Mix until thoroughly combined, about 2 minutes.

Grease and line two 9-inch cake pans with waxed paper. Pour the batter into the pans and bake at 350°F for 35–40 minutes, or until done. Test with a toothpick; if it comes out clean, the cake is done. Cool cake in the pans for 10 minutes, then turn out onto cooling racks. Once the cake has cooled completely, fill and frost with whipped cream.

CREAM CAKE, VANILLA CREAM SAUCE ❧

This cake recipe has "vanilla" in its title because the common flavoring of the time was lemon. Vanilla was not commonly used until much later because it was not readily available and so was a special treat. This recipe was adapted from *One Thousand and One Useful Recipes and Valuable Hints About Cooking and Housekeeping.*

MAKES 1 CAKE

---

2 eggs

¾ cup light cream

1 cup sugar

1½ cups flour

½ teaspoon salt

½ teaspoon baking soda

2½ teaspoons baking powder

1 teaspoon vanilla extract

Vanilla Cream Sauce (recipe follows)

Preheat oven to 350°F.

Combine eggs, cream, and sugar in a large bowl; whip until light.

In a smaller bowl, sift the flour, salt, baking soda, and baking powder. Add the sifted ingredients and vanilla to the eggs and cream. Mix well.

Pour the batter into a 9-inch cake pan that has been greased and floured. Bake at 350°F for 25–30 minutes. Check with a toothpick for doneness. Allow the cake to cool in the pan for 5 minutes; remove from the pan and cool completely on a cake rack. Once the cake has cooled, slice it in half to make two layers; fill with vanilla cream sauce.

VANILLA CREAM SAUCE ❧

MAKES 1 CUP

¾ cup heavy cream

¼ cup milk

¼ cup powdered sugar

½ teaspoon vanilla or lemon extract

Combine the cream and milk in a cold bowl; whip until stiff. Add the sugar and flavoring. Stir well.

CINNAMON STARS (ZIMTSTERNE), CIRCA 1880

Otto Geisenhofer was an early Tombstone baker and restaurateur who created many delicious baked goods for Tombstone's residents, and Christmas was extra special. These cookies appeared in his recipe book. This recipe was adapted from Otto Geisenhofer's original recipe, written in German, which was shared by his daughter.

MAKES ABOUT 30

4 egg whites

1½ cups sugar

2 teaspoons cinnamon

½ cup ground unpeeled almonds

¼ cup candied lemon peel

¼ cup candied orange peel

¼ teaspoon baking soda

1 cup flour for rolling

In a large bowl, beat the egg whites until soft peaks form (called *Schnee*, German for "snow"). Gradually add the sugar and cinnamon and continue beating until the egg whites are shining, about 10 minutes. Gently fold in the almonds, candied peels, and baking soda. Add enough of the flour to allow you to roll out the dough ¼ inch thick.

Cut with a star-shaped cookie cutter and place the cookies on a baking sheet lined with parchment paper. Allow the cookies to rest overnight.

The next day, bake the cookies at 325°F for 15 minutes.

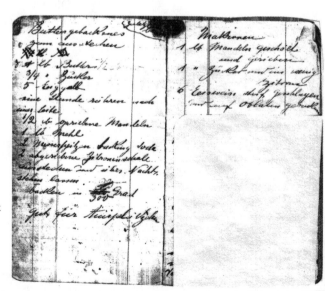

Otto's cookie recipe book in German, his native language
COURTESY OF THE GEISEN-HOFER FAMILY

BUTTER COOKIES FOR CUTTING (BUTTERGEBACKENES ZUM AUSSTECHEN), CIRCA 1880 ✑

This is another of Otto's traditional German Christmas cookie recipes from his own recipe collection. This recipe was adapted from Otto's original recipe, written in German, which was shared by his daughter.

MAKES 6 DOZEN 2-INCH-ROUND COOKIES

2 cups butter

⅔ cup sugar

2 egg yolks

Zest of 1 lemon

4 cups flour

½ cup ground almonds

1 teaspoon baking soda

Beat butter, sugar, and egg yolks for 20 minutes (this will give the batter volume); set aside. Add the remaining ingredients and blend well.

Roll dough out ½ inch thick. Cut out cookies and let them stand overnight.

The next day, bake on an ungreased cookie sheet at 300°F for 15 minutes.

GOOD WHITE GINGERBREAD COOKIES (GUILE WEISSE NÜRNBERGER LEBKUCKEN), CIRCA 1880 ✌

Tombstone had a couple of German bakers in town, and Christmastime was extra special with these traditional holiday cookies. This recipe was adapted from Otto Geisenhofer's original recipe, written in German, which was shared by his daughter.

MAKES 4 DOZEN 3-INCH COOKIES

1⅓ cups sugar

4 eggs

1 teaspoon cinnamon

¼ teaspoon ground cloves

¼ cup ground almonds

Peel of 1 lemon, finely diced

Juice of ½ lemon

¼ cup candied lemon peel

¼ cup candied orange peel

½ teaspoon baking soda

2 cups flour

Beat the sugar and eggs for 30 minutes until very thick and foamy. Add the remaining ingredients in the order given; mix well.

Put as much dough as you can handle on a floured board, roll it out, and cut it into shapes. Place cookies on cookie sheets greased with butter, but not too close together. Bake at 350°F for 10 minutes. Do not allow cookies to brown.

SPRINGERLE, CIRCA 1880 ✌

These cookies are made with a special rolling pin or cookie stamps that have fun or unique designs imprinted on them. As the cookies bake, they take on the shape of the imprint. This recipe was adapted from Otto Geisenhofer's original recipe, written in German, which was shared by his daughter.

MAKES ABOUT 2 DOZEN COOKIES

2½ cups flour

½ teaspoon baking powder

2 eggs

1⅓ cups sugar

3 teaspoons anise seeds

Peel of 1 lemon, finely chopped

Wooden forms or a patterned rolling pin

Sift the flour and baking powder together and set aside.

Beat eggs until thick. Gradually add sugar, and beat well until combined. Fold in the flour mixture, 2 teaspoons of the anise seeds, and the lemon peel. Mix well and then turn the dough out onto a heavily floured board to incorporate completely. Knead the dough only enough to make it the right consistency for rolling.

Roll the dough out until ½ inch thick. Press floured wooden forms or a patterned rolling pin on the dough so that the imprint shows clearly. Carefully remove the forms and use a dough cutter or knife to cut out the pieces.

Butter a baking sheet and sprinkle it with some flour and the remaining anise seeds. Place cookies on the baking sheet. The cookies must rest overnight before baking.

The next day, bake the cookies at 350°F for about 5 minutes. Do not allow them to brown.

ALMOND MACARONS (MAKRONEN), CIRCA 1880 ✑

Otto also made these cookies, which is his German version of the well-known French macarons. This recipe was adapted from Otto Geisenhofer's original recipe, written in German, which was shared by his daughter.

MAKES ABOUT 30

1 pound peeled almonds

6 egg whites

1 pound sugar

Zest of 1 lemon

Grind the almonds and set aside.

Place egg whites in a bowl and beat until soft peaks form. Gradually add the sugar and beat until stiff peaks form.

Gradually fold in the almonds and zest; mix with a spatula until smooth.

Drop tablespoons of batter onto a parchment-lined baking sheet, leaving about 2 inches between cookies. If you have a pastry bag, use a ½-inch plain tip.

Bake at 300°F for about 20 minutes, or until cookies are golden brown. Cool before serving.

VANILLA ICE CREAM ✎

In 1883 the French Bakery at 628 Fremont Street, Langpaap's at 515 Fremont, and J. M. Nash's Eclipse Bakery served the 6,300 people who called Tombstone home. Being close to the post office may have been advantageous for Frank Yaple and his ice-cream parlor. As people came and went to get their parcels and letters, the delightful aromas from his freshly made candy and ice cream may have been a sweet temptation. This recipe was adapted from *One Thousand and One Useful Recipes and Valuable Hints About Cooking and Housekeeping*.

MAKES 4 QUARTS

---

2 cups sugar

1 pint milk

1 teaspoon cornstarch

1 egg, beaten well

1 quart heavy cream

1 teaspoon vanilla

Heat sugar, milk, cornstarch, and egg in a large saucepan over low heat. Stir to combine, and cook until cornstarch has dissolved; let cool. Once cooled, add the cream and vanilla. Strain into an ice-cream machine, and freeze according to machine instructions.

CHOCOLATE ICE CREAM ✑

Franklin "Frank" Yaple was a New York native who lived in Virginia City, Nevada, in 1880 before coming to Tombstone. He was an agent for the Singer Sewing Machine Co. there and brought that business to Tombstone in 1881. In late 1882 he entered the ice cream and candy business, offering those treats to Tombstonians for years to come. He was one of the pioneers who stuck it out in town and lived there until he died in 1916. He's buried in Tombstone's City Cemetery. He advertised: "The finest lines of candies in the Territory. Ice cream and toys in their season." This recipe was adapted from California's *Petaluma Weekly Argus*, October 8, 1887.

MAKES 4 QUARTS

2 cups sugar

1 pint milk

1 teaspoon cornstarch

1 egg, well beaten

8 ounces dark chocolate

1 quart heavy cream

1 teaspoon vanilla

Heat sugar, milk, cornstarch, egg, and chocolate in a large saucepan over medium-low heat. Stir to combine, and cook until the chocolate has melted; let cool. Once cooled, add the cream and vanilla. Pour mixture into ice-cream machine, and freeze according to machine instructions.

Frank Yaple was one of the best confectioners in Tombstone.
SOUTHERN PACIFIC COAST DIRECTORY, 1888–1889

STRAWBERRY ICE CREAM ✌

Mother Nature was not too kind to Tombstone in 1887, when Tombstone's residents and buildings were shaken by an earthquake in early May. Ernest Storm and C. S. Abbott reported that a rush of water flooded the Sulphur Springs Valley. They also reported that about 1½ miles from Abbott's house, water shot out of the ground, reaching a height of 4 or 5 feet and extending about 100 feet in distance. Fortunately, other than a few cracked walls, Tombstone was barely affected by the sudden quake.

The ladies of the Methodist church certainly did not let a little thing like an earthquake get in the way of their fundraising activities, and on May 5 they held a strawberry and ice-cream festival to raise funds for the parsonage. The fundraiser was reported to be a "grand success, both socially and financially." This recipe was adapted from Los Angeles's *Evening Express*, June 30, 1890.

MAKES 4 QUARTS

2 cups sugar

1 pint milk

1 teaspoon cornstarch

1 egg, beaten well

1 quart heavy cream

1 teaspoon vanilla

2 cups pureed strawberries

Heat sugar, milk, cornstarch, and egg in a large saucepan over medium-low heat. Stir to combine, and cook until cornstarch has dissolved; let cool. Once cooled, add the cream, vanilla, and strawberry puree. Pour mixture into ice-cream machine, and freeze according to machine instructions.

INDIAN PUDDING ✎

California continued to be the primary source of the merchandise arriving in Tombstone, and the town's merchants were quick to advertise what would be arriving. Russel Mansfield advertised fresh cranberries, and Joe Hoefler announced that Louisiana molasses was available for $1.25 a gallon. Dyar and Baldwin's sold fine Sonora oranges at 35 cents a dozen, while Messick and Wolcott were offering a "choice lot" of dried fruit, eastern oatmeal, hominy, dried beef, and Pioneer Mills flour, along with comb and extract honey. Grocers sold milk, but it was condensed. Those wanting fresh milk to make delicious desserts like this purchased it from Abbott and Peck's dairy farm just outside of town. This recipe was adapted from the *Tombstone Epitaph*, July 26, 1890.

SERVES 4–6

---

4 cups milk, scalded

¾ cup cornmeal

⅓ cup sugar

1 teaspoon salt

5 teaspoons butter

½ cup molasses

Place cornmeal in a large double boiler or a metal bowl over simmering water. Slowly pour the milk over the cornmeal. Stir to combine, and allow to cook for 20 minutes. Add the sugar, salt, butter, and molasses. Stir.

Pour into a buttered baking dish and bake at 275°F for 2 hours. Remove from the oven and beat the pudding with a whisk to combine. Return the pudding to the oven and bake 1 additional hour. The pudding may also be poured into 6 small ramekins and baked for about the same time. Serve warm.

LEMON CUSTARD PUDDING ✌

Even though Tombstone was stable, its food industry was very cyclical. In 1884 it would have been a challenge for a diner to go back to an eatery the following year and find the same owner or cook. For example, Nellie Cashman owned the Grand Restaurant where Armand Tuquet was preparing meals, but he soon left to become the proud owner of the Maison Doree, where he offered oysters, chicken, turkey, wild game, pudding, pies, etc. This recipe was adapted from Marion Harland's *Breakfast, Luncheon and Tea*, 1875.

SERVES 2–4

5 egg yolks

⅓ cup powdered sugar

1½ cups whole milk

Grated peel of 1 lemon

Juice of 1 lemon

2 egg whites

3 tablespoons powdered sugar

Beat the egg yolks and sugar in a bowl until light yellow in color.

Scald the milk in a saucepan over medium heat; slowly add the egg yolks, stirring constantly. Add the lemon juice and grated peel, and bring to a boil; cook for 1 minute, stirring constantly.

Pour into a buttered ovenproof casserole or individual custard cups. Place in another container and fill with water so that it comes halfway up the sides of the casserole or custard cups. Bake at 325°F for about 30 minutes, or until set. A knife inserted will come out clean when the custard is done.

While custard is baking, beat the egg whites in a bowl until stiff. Gradually add the 3 tablespoons powdered sugar. Spread the whites on top of the cooked custard and put back in the oven until the top is golden.

QUEEN CHARLOTTE PUDDING ❧

By the fall of 1887, six months after the earthquake Tombstone was ready to enjoy Thanksgiving again. People went to private parties, had quiet family gatherings, and dined out. The Maison Doree continued the tradition of serving the usual turkey dinner with all the trimmings, along with fish, regular dinner entrees, vegetables, and fancy desserts. This recipe was adapted from Tucson's *Arizona Weekly Star*, January 4, 1883.

SERVES 4–6

---

2 cups fine breadcrumbs

2 cups milk

1½ cups sugar

4 egg yolks, beaten

Grated peel of 1 lemon

4 egg whites

Juice of 1 lemon

Jelly of your choice

In a large bowl, combine the breadcrumbs, milk, ½ cup of the sugar, egg yolks, and lemon peel; stir well. Pour mixture into a deep baking dish and bake at 350°F for 45–50 minutes, or until no longer watery.

In a separate bowl, beat the egg whites until stiff. Gradually add the remaining 1 cup sugar and the lemon juice to the whites.

Spread a layer of your favorite jelly over the baked pudding, then pour the egg whites over the jelly. Bake in a 350°F oven just until the top browns lightly.

Allow to cool slightly before placing in the refrigerator; chill for at least 4 hours.

LEMON PIE ✑

Longtime merchant Frank Wolcott needed to initiate a new policy and started selling strictly for cash at his grocery store. This enabled him to offer his customers a better rate on their purchases because he no longer needed to mark up his prices to cover unpaid debts. Some of Wolcott's items, like lemons, came from California and Arizona and were often used in delicious desserts. This recipe was adapted from Robin Andrews's *Lena's Little Red Book of Cake Recipes*.

MAKES 1 PIE

1¼ cups sugar

5⅓ tablespoons cornstarch

1½ cups hot water

3 eggs, separated

3 tablespoons butter

4 tablespoons lemon juice

1½ tablespoons grated lemon rind

1 piecrust, prebaked

Meringue (see recipe on page 159)

Combine the sugar, cornstarch, and water in a large saucepan. Cook over medium-high heat until the mixture begins to boil and thicken. Remove from the heat.

In a small bowl, beat the egg yolks until thick and lemon colored. Gradually add 3 tablespoons of the cooked mixture to the egg yolks, and stir well. Now add the egg yolks to the saucepan and incorporate. Cook over medium-high heat for about 1 minute, stirring constantly. Add the butter, lemon juice, and lemon peel.

Pour mixture into the prebaked pie shell and top with meringue. Bake at 375°F for 10–15 minutes, or until the meringue becomes golden.

PIECRUST ❧

This was often referred to in old recipe books as pie paste. This piecrust can be used for either the sweet or savory pie recipes in this book. This recipe was created by the author based on typical 1800s recipes.

MAKES 1 DOUBLE 9-INCH PIECRUST

---

2 cups flour

1½ teaspoons baking powder

¼ teaspoon salt

1 cup cold butter or shortening

1 egg

¼ teaspoon vinegar

Cold water

Combine the flour, baking powder, and salt in a large mixing bowl. Stir with a wire whisk to combine. Cut in the butter or shortening with a pastry cutter until the dough resembles crumbs.

Break the egg into a liquid measuring cup and beat lightly. Add the vinegar and enough water to measure ⅓ cup. Stir well. Add liquid to the flour and shortening mixture. Stir only enough to moisten and combine; overmixing will result in a tough crust. If the dough seems too wet, add a little more flour.

Divide the dough in half and roll out on a floured surface.

Note: To make a sweeter crust, add 1 tablespoon sugar and ½ teaspoon cinnamon to the flour mix. You can cut this recipe in half to make a single crust.

GREEN APPLE DUMPLINGS WITH BRANDY SAUCE ✌

Don't let the name "green apple" throw you off. Remember, in the 1880s "green" referred to fruit that was fresh and not dried. These dumplings were a special treat for Tombstone diners. This recipe was adapted from San Francisco's *The Daily Examiner*, April 1, 1879.

MAKES 6

6 large apples, peeled and cored

1 tablespoon lemon juice

¾ teaspoon cinnamon

¼ teaspoon salt

4 tablespoons butter

4 tablespoons brown sugar

1 double piecrust (see recipe on page 154)

Brandy Sauce (see next page)

Brush the apples with the lemon juice to prevent them from turning brown.

In a small bowl, combine the remaining ingredients except the piecrust; blend well.

Roll the piecrust dough on a floured surface to ⅛ inch thick. Cut into squares large enough to wrap around the apples.

Place the apples on the squares and fill the centers with the sugar filling. Bring the corners of the dough up to the center and pinch the seams closed.

Bake on a greased baking sheet at 350°F for 25–30 minutes, or until the apples are tender. Serve warm, topped with brandy sauce.

BRANDY SAUCE ✑

MAKES 1 CUP

½ cup butter

1 cup powdered sugar

1 egg, beaten

2 tablespoons hot water

2 tablespoons brandy

Beat the butter and sugar together in a saucepan over medium heat until light and fluffy. Stir in the egg and water; continue stirring while the sauce starts to thicken. Add the brandy and cook for 1 minute.

RAISIN PIE ❧

Raisin pie was also called funeral pie because it was often served at funeral wakes and likely originated with the Amish and Mennonites. Dried fruits were very popular, since produce wasn't readily available like it is today. As they used to say in Tombstone, "Give it a trial." This recipe was adapted from San Francisco's *Daily Examiner*, January 7, 1883.

MAKES 1 PIE

⅓ cup lemon juice

1 teaspoon grated lemon peel

½ cup orange juice

2 teaspoons grated orange peel

1 cup brown sugar

2 cups raisins

1¼ cup water

6 tablespoons flour

½ cup brandy

1 double piecrust (see recipe on page 154)

Combine the lemon juice, lemon peel, orange juice, orange peel, brown sugar, raisins, and water in a saucepan and bring to a boil.

In a small bowl, combine the flour and brandy. The mixture should resemble a smooth paste. Gradually add this to the raisin mixture, stirring constantly. Cook over high heat for 5 minutes.

Line a 9-inch pie pan with the bottom crust and add the raisin mixture. Cover with the second crust, and flute the edges. Bake at 400°F for 40 minutes.

COCONUT CREAM PIE ๑๑

In 1889 the *Daily Tombstone Epitaph* wrote a fun story about the Can Can Restaurant. They reported: "The waiter bawled throughout the hall, 'We do not give bread with one fishball!' This little bit of doggerel is not applicable to the Can Can, as they don't furnish that kind of 'chuck on Sunday, but they do dish up chicken done to a turn (whatever that means), but juiciest of meats, ice cream, cocoanut and custard pie and other palatable trimmings for the inner man and woman." This recipe was adapted from *Lena's Little Red Book of Cake Recipes* by Robin Andrews.

MAKES 1 PIE

½ cup sugar

⅓ cup flour

½ teaspoon salt

½ cup milk

½ cup butter, melted

3 egg yolks

½ teaspoon vanilla

1 heaping cup shredded coconut

1 9-inch pie shell, baked

Mix flour, sugar, flour, salt, milk, butter, and egg yolks in large saucepan. Cook over medium heat, stirring constantly until thick. Remove from the heat and stir in the vanilla and coconut.

Pour mixture into the baked piecrust. Gently spread filling to edges to seal well. Sprinkle additional coconut on top.

Bake at 325°F for 10 minutes, or until top is golden. Refrigerate until completely cold before serving.

MERINGUE ✑

3 egg whites	Whip egg whites until foamy; add the sugar. Continue beating on high speed until semi-stiff peaks form.
¼ cup sugar	

BLACKBERRY PIE ✑

Even though merchants Fitzhenry and Mansfield were doing well, John Fitzhenry left the business and Tombstone, but his partner, Russel Mansfield, remained in town. He continued to offer Tombstone a variety of goods, including the usual selection of fine teas and coffees, as well as pure maple syrup. William Head, another merchant, sold fresh ranch butter, eggs, berries, and garden vegetables "at the lowest cash prices" at his Family Grocery Store on 312 Allen Street. When fresh berries were in season or brought to Tombstone, restaurant menus often included pies. This recipe was adapted from Arizona's *Phoenix Herald*, June 14, 1879.

MAKES 1 PIE

---

3 cup fresh blackberries

1 cup sugar

2 tablespoons flour

2 tablespoons lemon juice

1 tablespoon butter, cut into pieces

1 double piecrust (see recipe on page 154)

Combine the berries, sugar, flour, and lemon juice in a large bowl. Gently toss the mixture to coat the berries evenly.

Pour mixture into a 9-inch pie pan lined with one crust; dot the fruit with butter and cover with the second piecrust. Cut 3 or 4 holes in the crust to allow the steam to escape.

Bake at 350°F for 35–40 minutes, or until the berries are tender. Allow to cool for 30 minutes before cutting. Serve with whipped cream and freshly grated nutmeg.

CUSTARD PIE ✑

Diners perusing the *Daily Tombstone* newspaper saw ads in 1885 for Mrs. Holland's California Restaurant, Jacob Everhardy's Fremont Street Meat Market, Joseph Stumpf's American Bakery, Freeman and Coleman's Pacific Chop House, and Pauline Jones's International Restaurant on Allen Street. Pauline's new chef de cuisine was Louis Roge, late of the Grand Restaurant. Harry Wisdom announced his Fountain Restaurant on Allen had been renovated, painted, and thoroughly refitted, and boasted it was one of the "neatest places in town to get a meal." He offered his patrons a good variety of breakfast, lunch, and dinner entrees that included fresh pumpernickel bread, rock cod, tomcod, sea bass, and Spanish mackerel. The fish served for breakfast at the Fountain had been packed in ice and shipped by express from California. He also tempted diners by claiming his restaurant was the coolest place in town to have a meal because there was no smoke, heat, or smell from the kitchen, which was entirely separate from the dining room. They served their customers nothing but the choicest steaks, cutlets, chops, fish, game, and oysters, along with ranch eggs and buttermilk. This recipe was adapted from *One Thousand and One Useful Recipes and Valuable Hints About Cooking and Housekeeping*.

MAKES 1 PIE

---

3 eggs

3 tablespoons sugar

⅛ teaspoon salt

1¼ cups milk

Nutmeg, freshly grated

1 8-inch piecrust (see recipe on page 154)

In a large bowl, beat the eggs. Add the sugar, salt, and milk; beat until light and fluffy.

Pour the custard into the piecrust and sprinkle the top with freshly grated nutmeg. Bake at 450°F for 10 minutes; reduce heat to 350°F and continue cooking for an additional 50 minutes, or until a knife inserted comes out clean.

Allow pie to cool completely before cutting. Chilling the pie enhances the flavors.

PEACH PIE ✌

The Russ House's chief cook was Ben Wurtmann in 1885, and he continued to offer impressive bills of fare to his patrons. In November he offered pumpkin, apple, mince, and peach pies. This recipe was adapted from *One Thousand and One Useful Recipes and Valuable Hints About Cooking and Housekeeping.*

MAKES 1 PIE

½ cup light brown sugar

¼ teaspoon salt

2 tablespoons flour

½ cup honey

6 large peaches, peeled and cut into ⅛-inch slices

2 tablespoons cold butter, cut into pieces

1 double piecrust (see recipe on page 154)

Whipped cream or vanilla ice cream

Combine the brown sugar, salt, and flour in a large bowl. Stir in the honey and mix well. Add the peaches and toss to coat evenly.

Pour mixture into a 9-inch pie pan that has been lined with one crust. Dot the filling with the butter bits, and cover with the second crust. Make 3 or 4 slits in the top of the pie.

Bake at 450°F for 15 minutes. Reduce heat to 350°F and bake an additional 35 minutes, or until the peaches are tender. If the piecrust edges begin to brown too much, cover them with aluminum foil.

Allow pie to cool for 30 minutes before cutting. Serve with whipped cream or vanilla ice cream.

CREAM PIE ✌

Jacob Everhardy may have been Tombstone's butcher, but he also took milk orders for residents who wanted it in 1885. Five people offered milk to residents: Gilbert & Braly, Mrs. H. C. Herrick, N. Van Alstine, S. C. Roberston, and Antonio Edmunds. The cost of milk was 40 cents per gallon and 12½ cents per quart. Mrs. Herrick would only deliver once per day and also sold milk to the city for the county hospital. Milk was used to make this recipe, which was adapted from *Lena's Little Red Book of Cake Recipes* by Robin Andrews.

MAKES 1 PIE

---

1 cup sugar

⅓ cup flour

¼ teaspoon salt

2 eggs, well beaten

2 cups milk, scalded

1 teaspoon vanilla extract

½ teaspoon lemon extract

1 8-inch piecrust, prebaked

Combine dry ingredients in a large metal bowl. Stir in eggs and milk and blend well. Place the bowl over a pot of simmering water (or use a double boiler). Cook the mixture for 15 minutes, stirring constantly, until thickened. Check your heat—you do not want to scramble the eggs. Cool mixture; add the vanilla and lemon extracts.

Pour the cream filling into the prebaked piecrust. Dust with powdered sugar and garnish with mint leaves and berries.

The pie should be served immediately. If you allow it to sit too long, it will become soggy.

APRICOT FRIED PIES ✑

Tombstone residents would have been excited to see the fruit crop report in the *Epitaph* in May 1887. San Francisco fruit merchants were happy to announce that the peach and apricot crops were exceedingly large. This recipe was adapted from *Scammell's Cyclopedia of Valuable Receipts*.

MAKES 4–6 HAND PIES

6 ounces dried apricots or cherries

Water

¾ cup sugar

1 piecrust (see recipe on page 154)

Oil for frying

Place dried fruit in a medium saucepan and add water just to cover. Bring to a boil over high heat; cook until the fruit is tender and the water has evaporated.

Add the sugar and cook for another 2–3 minutes. Remove fruit from the heat and mash. Cool.

Roll out piecrust to ¼-inch thickness; cut into 6-inch circles or whatever size is desired. Place a tablespoon of the fruit on one side of the piecrust circle. Moisten the circle with water and fold it in half. Use a fork to seal the edges.

Add enough oil to a large stockpot to come up ½ inch and heat over medium-high heat. Test the oil by adding a small piece of leftover piecrust. If it bubbles, the oil is ready. Gently add the pies, 3 at a time, with tongs. Cook for about 2 minutes on one side; turn pies over and cook until golden. Drain on paper towels. ***Caution:*** Filling will be hot.

SQUASH PIE ✑

Nellie Cashman, who served many a pie in Tombstone, moved to Nogales, Arizona Territory, in 1885. She was joined by Pauline Jones, who sold her International Restaurant to Alexander Rossi and Joseph Micotti of Tucson. The two women left Tombstone with plans to open their own hotel and restaurant in Nogales. Cashman's Russ House was leased to Mrs. T. S. (Mary) O'Brien, who kept chief cook Ben Wurtmann. Later in the year, O'Brien left the Russ House and opened the Arcade Restaurant at Cadwell and Stanford's former location.

Nellie Cashman never came back to live in Tombstone, but Pauline did after her restaurant burned down in 1892. She returned to Tombstone in 1893 and took over the Maison Doree, but left a year later to begin a business in San Francisco. However, after Pauline insured her lodging house, she set fire to it on the advice of a bad partner. She ended up okay and three years later married a man named Chris Eisele, who owned a large lodging house in Spokane Falls, Washington. This recipe was adapted from San Francisco's *Daily Examiner*, November 1, 1885.

MAKES 1 PIE

1 cup sugar

3 eggs, beaten

1 cup cooked and mashed squash or zucchini, drained

¾ teaspoon salt

1 teaspoon cinnamon

1 teaspoon freshly grated nutmeg

1 cup evaporated milk

1 piecrust (see recipe on page 154)

In a medium bowl, combine the ingredients, except for the piecrust, in the order given. Be sure to stir thoroughly after each addition. Pour into a 9-inch pie pan lined with the single piecrust.

Bake at 450°F for 10 minutes. Reduce the temperature to 350°F and bake 40 minutes more. The pie will be done when a knife inserted in it comes out clean.

APPLE PIE ✵

Merchant Joe Hoefler changed the name of his business to the Pioneer Store in 1887. He still carried a variety of general merchandise, but also specialized in agricultural supplies for ranchers and miners. Frank Wolcott still sold groceries like fresh ranch butter, fresh fish, and eastern oysters every Thursday. Other imported goods such as French peas, Italian mushrooms, Tuscan olive oil, and Swiss cheese could be purchased from the Old French Market at the corner of Allen and 6th Streets. This recipe was adapted from the 1872 *California Recipe Book*.

MAKES 1 PIE

---

1 double piecrust (see recipe on page 154)

4–6 tart apples, peeled, cored, and sliced

¼–½ cup sugar (to taste)

½ teaspoon cinnamon

¼ teaspoon salt

¼ cup flour

Butter, cut into ¼-inch squares

Line a 9- or 10-inch pie pan with one crust.

Combine apples, sugar, cinnamon, salt, and flour in a bowl. Stir to coat the apples evenly. Put the apple mixture in the piecrust. Place a few pieces of butter around the pie, and cover with the second crust.

Bake for about 40 minutes at 350°F, or until the apples are tender. Serve with ice cream or whipped cream.

CREAM PUFFS ✤

Cream puffs were a popular item during the nineteenth century. Some recipes of the time called for either a whipped cream or pastry cream filling, so the choice is yours! This recipe was adapted from *Lena's Little Red Book of Cake Recipes* by Robin Andrews.

MAKES 36

½ cup butter

½ teaspoon salt

1 cup water

1 cup flour

4 eggs

Powdered sugar

Whipped Cream Filling (see recipe on page 130) or

Pastry Cream Filling (see recipe on page 126)

In a large saucepan, bring the butter, salt, and water to a boil over high heat. Once it begins to boil, reduce the heat to low and add the flour. Stir vigorously until the dough forms a ball and clings to the spoon. Remove from heat and allow to sit for 5–10 minutes to cool slightly. Add eggs to cooled dough, one at a time. Beat thoroughly after each addition. After the last egg has been added, continue beating until the dough becomes thick and shiny.

Place tablespoonfuls of dough 2 inches apart on an ungreased baking sheet. Bake at 425°F for 10 minutes; reduce heat to 375°F and bake an additional 20 minutes. Make a small slit in the side of each puff and place back in the oven for about 10 minutes so the steam can escape. Cool completely.

Remove the tops and fill puffs with whipped cream or pastry cream. Replace tops and dust with powdered sugar.

Note: These do not sit well for very long and should be eaten shortly after they've been prepared.

QUEEN FRITTERS, VANILLA FLAVOR ✒

Butter was an important ingredient in many of Tombstone's dishes, and there was a growing concern that some butters were not the genuine article. The fear was not that Tombstone merchants were tampering with the butter, but some in Tucson and Prescott were. The *Epitaph* noted that butter could be tested for purity by putting a few drops of sulfuric acid on cream butter. If it turned pure white, the butter was real. If the butter had been colored yellow artificially, it would turn dark red. Animal or vegetable fat used to manufacture "butter" would give it a rainbow color. This recipe was adapted from California's *Sacramento Daily Record-Union*, June 14, 1884.

SERVES 4

¼ cup butter

½ cup water

½ cup flour

2 eggs

1 teaspoon vanilla

Oil for frying

Jelly or jam

Powdered sugar

Place the butter and water in a medium saucepan over high heat. Once the water begins to boil, add the flour. Continue stirring until the flour mixture begins to pull away from the saucepan's sides. Remove from heat. Add the eggs one at a time, beating thoroughly after each addition. Add vanilla and stir.

In a large Dutch oven, melt enough oil to deep-fry the fritters. Gently drop the batter by spoonfuls, and cook until golden brown and puffy. Drain fritters on a paper towel.

Remove a small section of the top of the fritter and fill with your favorite jam or jelly. Dust with powdered sugar.

CHARLOTTE DES POMMES ✒

This Apple Charlotte is an especially tasty dessert, and it's not as complicated as you might think. It was a great way for Tombstone cooks to use not-so-fresh bread. This recipe was adapted from San Francisco's *Daily Examiner*, March 24, 1880.

SERVES 4–6

4 quarts apples, peeled and sliced ⅛ inch thick

½ cup apricot preserves

⅔ cup sugar

3 tablespoons butter

2 teaspoons vanilla extract

¼ cup dark rum

12 slices firm bread, ¼ inch thick

¾ cup butter, melted

For the Glaze:

½ cup strained apricot jam

3 tablespoons dark rum

2 tablespoons sugar

Place the apples in a large skillet and cover. Cook over low heat for 20 minutes, stirring occasionally. The apples should be tender when done. Add the preserves, sugar, 2 tablespoons of the butter, and the vanilla. Cook over high heat, stirring constantly, until the mixture begins to thicken. Add rum. Remove from heat.

Remove crusts from the bread. Cut some of the bread into pieces to fit the bottom and sides of your mold. Brown these in remaining 1 tablespoon of butter and arrange in the mold. Cut the remaining bread into ½-inch-wide strips. Brush some of the strips heavily with the melted butter and line the mold with them. Make sure the strips overlap so there are no spaces in between.

Pour the apples into the mold and press down lightly. The apples should be mounded on top, as they will settle when cooking. Trim off any uneven bread. Cover the top with additional buttered bread strips. Thoroughly brush the top again with melted butter.

Place the mold on a baking sheet and bake at 425°F for 30 minutes. Cool in the mold for 15 minutes. Turn out onto a serving platter by lifting the mold slowly off the charlotte. If the dessert starts to collapse, set the mold down and try again in 5 minutes.

To make the glaze: Place the jam, 3 tablespoons rum, and 2 tablespoons sugar in a saucepan; boil until thick. Brush the charlotte with the glaze. This can be served hot or cold.

ENGLISH PLUM PUDDING ✑

This dessert is an old tradition from England, but it appeared on menus and tables across the frontier, including the Maison Doree restaurant in the Cosmopolitan Hotel. It was served with a variety of sauces, including brandy, hard, or lemon. This recipe is from Sarah Hescox, who was my fifth great-grandmother and came to America from England in 1832. "Being ye ancient recipe used by grandmother Hescox and handed down through ye good grandmother Wilkins to grandma Whippy, ma Turner and the Osgoods." Generational recipes were cherished and a part of every woman's collection when she became a wife. They took them wherever they traveled.

SERVES 6

---

2 cups stale bread

2 cups milk

1 egg, beaten

¼ cup molasses

¼ cup sugar

6 tablespoons butter, melted

½ cup raisins, prunes, or a combination

½ teaspoon salt

¼ teaspoon cinnamon

¼ teaspoon cloves

¼ teaspoon mace (an additional ⅛ teaspoon nutmeg can be substituted for mace)

¼ nutmeg, grated

½ teaspoon chopped orange peel

1 cup brandy

Remove the crusts from the bread; cut or shred the bread into small pieces and lay on a baking sheet. Bake at 300°F until dry—about 10 minutes, depending on how dry the bread was to start. Place the bread in a large bowl and cover with the milk. Let stand for about 1 hour, or until the milk is absorbed and bread is soft.

Beat the bread and milk until combined; add the egg, molasses, sugar, butter, raisins, salt, spices, and orange peel.

Grease a 2-quart ovenproof dish. Fill with the batter, but stop about an inch or two from the top. Cover with a lid or heavy-duty aluminum foil. Bake at 300°F for 2 hours. Test with a knife; if it comes out clean when put into center of pudding, it's done.

Pour brandy over the pudding and allow to cool. Refrigerate until ready to eat.

When ready to serve, warm additional brandy and ignite. Serve while flaming.

TOMBSTONE SLOWS DOWN

When 1887 arrived, only a couple mines were operating, and only on a small scale. Businesses remained open, but their numbers diminished. Those that did stay included many of Tombstone's early pioneers. Supplies still arrived to support them, and the newspapers advertised that large quantities of freight were still arriving in town and would be available to the public. Items such as wine, liquors, food products, cigars, toiletries, and clothing were included in these shipments. When 1887 ended there was a strong hope that Tombstone would somehow get back to the life it once knew. Only a few changes took place in 1888, and eight restaurants, including the Can Can, Elite, Russ House, Occidental, Gregory's, Maison Doree, and the Pacific Chop House, remained. Otto Geisenhofer renamed his business the New York Restaurant, where he sold meals for 25 cents on Allen Street until he left two years later. The only two bakeries were operated by W. D. Coleman, onetime owner of the Pacific Chop House, and R. A. Woodbury. Frank Yaple's confectionery and ice-cream store continued to serve tempting treats. The butchers, which had numbered approximately eleven four years earlier, now totaled four, including Apollinar Bauer's Pioneer Meat Market. Tombstone had been accustomed to a variety of large mercantile firms, but by 1888 there were mostly small shops, except for Frank Wolcott. Wolcott was still importing oysters to Tombstone by first-class mail; they were so popular, he could not keep them in stock. Despite all that, well-known business people like Nellie Cashman, Joseph Pascholy, Frank Yaple, and Otto Geisenhofer left the following year. Pascholy left after a fire destroyed his Occidental Hotel in September 1888. He opened a hotel in Huachuca, Arizona, in 1890. Despite the turmoil, and Tombstone's economic slowdown, many residents and business owners were determined to stay. Otto spent ten years of his life in Tombstone before leaving in 1889. From Tombstone he went to nearby Bisbee, where he purchased the Waldorf Hotel and also ran his own butcher shop. He soon married a French woman and moved to San Leandro, California, with his new bride because, he said, "Arizona was no place for a lady."

Mining, the driving force behind Tombstone, continued on a very small scale, which allowed Tombstone to remain in existence. Residents refused to give up the dream of being the most prosperous town in Arizona. To remain that way, they tried to lure people to town for reasons other than mining. They claimed, and rightly so, that Tombstone was a well-planned town with broad streets where the climate was healthful, with warm summer days and cool, pleasant nights. Their water was clear, sparkling, and sweet. Despite their efforts, people continued to leave Tombstone for something better, and its population steadily declined. But during its heyday, Tombstone offered a variety of places to eat, from boardinghouses to fine dining establishments.

APPENDIX: TOMBSTONE BUSINESSES

Some businesses used the same names over the years but were completely different establishments. This list includes entries for the chefs who could be identified; "owners'" names are those who owned the business, not necessarily the land or the building. Businesses often leased space from the owners. This list also includes other food-related business. Some details were easier to locate than others, so some may not have a complete history. This is not an all-inclusive list of all the businesses, only the ones mentioned in this book.

HOTELS

AMERICAN HOUSE HOTEL, 427–429 FREMONT STREET
Nellie Cashman and Frances "Fannie" Cunningham, 1882

BROWN'S HOTEL, CORNER 4TH AND ALLEN STREETS (ORIGINALLY MOJAVE)
Charles Brown, 1879–1882 (lost to fire)

COSMOPOLITAN HOTEL, 407–411 ALLEN STREET
Carl Gustav Bilicke and son, Albert Bilicke, 1879–1882 (lost to fire)

GRAND HOTEL, 424–426 ALLEN STREET
John and Lavina Holly, 1880–1881

Jessie Brown, 1881–1882

Archie and Fannie McBride, 1882 (lost to fire)

LEVAN HOUSE, 533–535 ALLEN STREET
William and Isabelle "Belle" LeVan, 1882–1884

MELROSE LODGINGS HOUSE, 617 FREMONT STREET
Mrs. M. L. Woods, 1882–1884

OCCIDENTAL HOTEL, CORNER 4TH AND ALLEN STREETS
Joseph Pascholy and Gottfried Tribolet, 1883–1884

Joseph Pascholy, 1884–1888

Joseph Pascholy and Anson P. K. Safford (first floors only after September 14, 1888; fire destroyed the hotel on the second floor), 1888

PALACE LODGING HOUSE, VARIOUS LOCATIONS

Miss Lucy Young, 5th Street, near Toughnut, 1882–1884

Mrs. D. B. Immel, corner 5th and Toughnut Streets, 1884–1885 (she died)

Mrs. Henriette Bastian (opened Hotel Arlington), 1886–1894

Mrs. S. Gallen (changed name to Palace Hotel, now on 5th Street), 1894–1896

RESTAURANTS

AMERICAN RESTAURANT, ALLEN, BETWEEN 6TH AND 7TH STREETS

Mrs. S. J. Dill, 1882–1884

Mrs. Pierce, 1886

ARCADE, 507 ALLEN STREET

Nellie Cashman, October 1880–May 1881

Julius Albert Koska, May–June 1881 (lost to fire)

BAYLEY'S RESTAURANT (IN BROWN'S HOTEL), 403 ALLEN STREET

George Bayley, 1880–1881

BON TON RESTAURANT, 321 ALLEN STREET

John Grattan, 1881

Mrs. Florence Hemsath, 1882

BOSS RESTAURANT, 605 ALLEN STREET

Jennie Harden, 1882

BOSTON HOUSE, 4TH STREET

Mrs. Merrill, 1880

BROOKLYN RESTAURANT, VARIOUS LOCATIONS

Captain John S. Young, 525 Allen Street, 1881 (lost to fire)

Joseph A. Bright (under LeVan House), 535 Allen Street, 1883

CALIFORNIA RESTAURANT, MULTIPLE LOCATIONS

George and Sophie Gregor, 715 Allen Street, 1883

Mrs. Holland, 6th Street, 1885

CAN CAN RESTAURANT, VARIOUS LOCATIONS

Andrew David Walsh and William W. Shanahan, 435 Allen Street, 1880–1881

A. D. Walsh & Co., 429 Allen Street, 1882–1887

John Watson, 419 Allen Street, 1887–1889

Andrew Walsh, corner of 4th and Allen Streets, 1889

Nellie Walsh, 1889 to mid-1890s

John Henninger, 1897–1900 (closed)

John Henninger, 1901–1906

Grace Lowry, 1906

John Henninger, 1906–1908 (Can Can merged with American Kitchen in 1908 to become Can Can Café). *Note: Ah Lum and Ah Sing, 1908–1919 (American Kitchen)*

Mrs. A Staninger, 1921

Mrs. Queenie Stumbo, 1922 (leased)

Mrs. E. R. Wagner, 1924

Various businesses in the building at 4th and Allen Streets, 1924–1929

Mrs. M. A. Fryer and son Kent, 1929

Mr. ? Jacobs, 1933–1934

CARLETON'S COFFEE, OYSTER, AND CHOP HOUSE, 523 ALLEN STREET

Frank Carleton, 1880

COSMOPOLITAN HOTEL DINING ROOM, 407–411 ALLEN STREET

Mr. Whitney, August 1880

Gustave Bilicke, August 1880

John O. Dunbar, August 1880

Mrs. Merrill, October 1880

J. W. Cameron, November–December 1880

CRYSTAL PALACE LUNCH PARLORS/CHOP HOUSE, VARIOUS LOCATIONS

Paul Neunkirch and Herman Golles, Allen Street, 1883

Fred Parker, 5th Street, 1885–1886

ELITE RESTAURANT/CHOP HOUSE, VARIOUS LOCATIONS

D. J. Bucksley, 215 Allen Street, 1881

Fred Parker and Mr. Burns, Allen Street, near 5th, 1886

Fred Parker, 1887

A. D. Cooley (owner; skipped town), Harry Wisdom (manager), 1888

Unknown, 1889

FOUNTAIN RESTAURANT/SALOON, ALLEN STREET, UNDER GRAND HOTEL

William B. Alderson and John Grattan, 1882

Harry Wisdom, Allen Street, between 4th and 5th, 1885–1886

GRAND HOTEL DINING ROOM/RESTAURANT, ALLEN STREET

Hotel owners, 1880–1881

Henry Holthower, 1881

Pauline Streckenbach, 1883

Nellie Cashman, 1884

GREGORY'S RESTAURANT, VARIOUS LOCATIONS

Thomas and Carrie Gregory, 410 Fremont Street, 1882–1886

Thomas Gregory, 316 Allen Street, 1887–1888

INTERNATIONAL RESTAURANT, 430 ALLEN STREET

Pauline Jones, 1882–1886

Mr. Alexander Rossi and Mr. Joseph Micotti, 1886–1887/1888

MAISON DOREE (FORMERLY COSMOPOLITAN), ALLEN STREET

George C. Marks, 1881

Louis Riche and Constantine Protopsaltis, 1881–1882 (destroyed in fire)

MAISON DOREE RESTAURANT, 5TH STREET BETWEEN ALLEN AND FREMONT; LATER 409 ALLEN STREET

Steve DeMartini, 1883

Armand and Amelia Tuquet, 1883–1891

Mr. Gamba, 1892

Pauline Jones, 1893 (Mr. and Mrs. Miller)

Julius Caesar, 1894

MELROSE RESTAURANT, 426 FREMONT STREET

Mrs. M. L. Woods, 1880–1881

James Noble, 1881

Edmund Saul, 1881

Jane Harding and Catherine Lang, 1881–1883

MODINI'S, ALLEN STREET, NEAR 6TH

George Modini, 1882

NEW ORLEANS RESTAURANT & LIQUOR SALOON, 219 4TH, 404 ALLEN, AND 514 ALLEN STREETS

Robert B. and Bridget Campbell, 1881 and 1882

T. A. and Pauline Jones, corner of 1st and Toughnut Streets, 1881–1883

NEW YORK COFFEE SALOON AND RESTAURANT, 203 4TH STREET

John L. McCullough, 1882–1884

OCCIDENTAL CHOP HOUSE, 429 ALLEN STREET

Aristotle Petro, 1881–1882

Peter Claudianos, 1882

OCCIDENTAL RESTAURANT (IN HOTEL), CORNER 4TH AND ALLEN STREETS

Jennie Harden, 1883–?

PACIFIC CHOP HOUSE, VARIOUS LOCATIONS

John L. McCullough and Tripp, Allen Street, between 4th and 5th, 1882–1883

Mr. Freeman and W. D. Coleman, 4th Street, between Allen and Fremont, 1885–1888

W. A. Anderson, Allen Street, between 3rd and 4th, 1888

ROCKAWAY OYSTER HOUSE/RESTAURANT, 207 5TH STREET

John Bogovich and M. Bruce, 1881–1882 (lost to fire)

John Bogovich & Co., 1883

RURAL HOUSE, 521 ALLEN STREET

John and Lavina Holly, January–June 1880

George Rutledge and James Crowley, June 1880–July 1880

James Crowley and Carrie Hanson, July 1880–October 1880

RUSS HOUSE, CORNER 5TH AND TOUGHNUT STREETS

Sol T. Anderson and Jacob Smith, 1880

Joseph Pascholy and Nellie Cashman, October 1881

Joseph Pascholy, 1882

Nellie Cashman, 1883

Frances "Fannie" Cunningham and Kate Ward, 1884

Mrs. Annie B. Paddock, August 1884 (leased)

Nellie Cashman, 1885

Mrs. T. S. (Mary) O'Brien, 1885 (leased), 1887–1890

STAR RESTAURANT,

Isaac "Ike" Clanton, located at the old mill site, 1878

Lucy Young and Belle Sullivan, 514 Allen, 1880

Mrs. Annie B. Paddock-Coyle, Allen between 5th and 6th, 1885

George Bauer, owner, Mrs. Bockman, manager, Allen between 5th and 6th, 1885–1886

ST. LOUIS RESTAURANT, 219 4TH STREET

Robert and Bridget Campbell, 1882

CHEFS/COOKS

LOUIS ALBRIGHT, GREGORY'S RESTAURANT, 1883

A. BERAENTHOL, INTERNATIONAL RESTAURANT, 1885

JOHN BOGOVICH, ROCKAWAY RESTAURANT, 1881–1883

HERMAN GOLLES, CRYSTAL PALACE CHOP HOUSE (BAKER), 1882–1883

JOHN GREGOR, CAN CAN RESTAURANT, 1887

HENRY HOLTHOWER, CAN CAN RESTAURANT, 1885

ISAAC "JAKEY" JACOBS, MAISON DOREE, 1881; PACIFIC CHOP HOUSE, 1882

MRS. MAGGIE MCGIVNEY, BROOKLYN RESTAURANT, 1883

GEORGE MANDICH, MAISON DOREE, 1883

PAUL NEUNKIRCH, CRYSTAL PALACE CHOP HOUSE (COOK), 1882–1883

EDWARD RAFFERTY, RUSS HOUSE, 1880

LOUIS RICHE

OCCIDENTAL CHOP HOUSE, 1881

MAISON DOREE, 1882

LOUIS ROGE, GRAND RESTAURANT, 1885

GEORGE RUTLEDGE, RURAL HOUSE, 1880

ARMAND TUQUET, MAISON DOREE, 1890

BENJAMIN WURTMANN

CAN CAN RESTAURANT, 1885

RUSS HOUSE, 1885

ALVAN S. YOUNG, OCCIDENTAL CHOP HOUSE, 1881, 1882

BAKERY/ICE CREAM/CONFECTIONERY

AMERICAN BAKERY, VARIOUS LOCATIONS

Joseph Stumpf, 215 5th Street, 1879–1887

A. D. Cooley and Mr. ? Turner, moved to 4th Street between Allen and Fremont, 1888

CITY BAKERY AND RESTAURANT, 529 ALLEN STREET

Otto Geisenhofer, 1879–1889

ECLIPSE BAKERY, FREMONT STREET

James Masters Nash, 1883–1885

FRENCH BAKERY, 628 FREMONT STREET

Unknown, 1881–1883

FOURTH STREET ICE CREAM PARLORS/BAKERY, VARIOUS LOCATIONS

Charles Langpaap, 535 Allen Street, 1882

Charles Langpaap, 515 Fremont Street, 1883

NEW YORK BAKERY, RESTAURANT AND COFFEE HOUSE, 415 ALLEN STREET

Julius and Sophie Caesar, 1881–1885

YAPLES, 76 5TH STREET

Frank Yaple, 1882–1889

MERCANTILE/GROCERS

CADWELL & STANFORD, 512 ALLEN STREET

Andrew I. Cadwell and Joseph A. Stanford, 1878–1884

CALIFORNIA VARIETY STORE, CORNER ALLEN AND 4TH STREETS

Michael Edwards, 1880

C.O.D. HOUSE, 328 FREMONT STREET

Chandler and Forsyth, 1882

DYAR, FINCH, AND BALDWIN/DYAR AND BALDWIN, 432 FREMONT STREET

Pascal M. Dyar, Calvin Luther Finch, and Washington Wellington Baldwin, 1883–1885

Pascal M. Dyar and Washington Wellington Baldwin (F. W. Cummings, manager), 1885–1886

Washington Wellington Baldwin, 1886

J. H. Hull, 1887

J. C. FITZHENRY'S/FITZHENRY & CO./FITZHENRY & MANSFIELD (AKA THE RED STORE), 217 5TH STREET

John C. Fitzhenry, 1881

John C. Fitzhenry and Russel P. Mansfield, 1881–1885

Russel P. Mansfield, The Red Store, 1885

HOEFLER'S/PIONEER STORE, VARIOUS LOCATIONS

Joseph Hoefler, 417 Allen, 1879–1882

Joseph Hoefler, 501 Fremont, 1882–1898

MCKEAN AND KNIGHT'S, CORNER 6TH AND ALLEN STREETS

James McKean and Isaac Knight, 1879–1881

F. A. MILICH & DYAR'S, 430–432 ALLEN STREET

Frank Anton Milich, 1881

Frank Anton Milich and Pascal M. Dyar, 1882

P. W. SMITH, CORNER 4TH AND ALLEN STREETS

P. W. Smith, 1879–1882

SHILLIAM'S, 4TH STREET, BETWEEN ALLEN AND FREMONT

William Shilliam, 1879

TASKER & PRIDHAM'S/PRIDHAM, MACNEIL & MOORE, CORNER 5TH AND ALLEN STREETS

Joseph Tasker and George Pridham, 1880–1882

George Pridham and Donald A. Macneil, 1882–1884

George Pridham, Donald A. Macneil, Frank Lester Moore, 1884

Donald A. Macneil and Frank Lester Moore, 1885

WOLCOTT'S, 414 FREMONT STREET

Frank N. Wolcott, 1883–1917 (shot in the Chiricahua Mountains)

WOODHEAD & GAY, 5TH STREET, NEAR FREMONT

Managed by Frank Wolcott, 1881–1883

MEAT MARKETS

CITY MEAT MARKET, 511 ALLEN STREET

Thomas Patrick Ward, 1880–1881

EAGLE MEAT MARKET (WAS COSMOPOLITAN), 5TH STREET

Abraham, Charles, Godfrey, Robert, and Siegfried Tribolet (Cosmopolitan), 1879

Godfrey Tribolet (Eagle), 1879

FREMONT STREET MEAT MARKET, VARIOUS LOCATIONS

Jacob Everhardy, 404 Fremont Street, 1881–1882

Lang, Everhardy & Co., 1882

J. Everhardy & Co., 428 Fremont Street, 1882

J. Everhardy & Co., 430 Fremont Street, 1885–1886

Mr. Sturges/Sturgis, 1886

HOOKER & BAUER'S, 4TH AND FREMONT STREETS

Apollinar Bauer and Henry Clay Hooker, 1880–1881

PIONEER MEAT MARKET, 4TH STREET, BETWEEN ALLEN AND FREMONT

Apollinar Bauer, 1886–1888

UNION POULTRY & MEAT MARKET, 318 FREMONT STREET

Bernard Bauer and James Kehoe, 1881–1882

UNION MEAT MARKET, 511 ALLEN STREET

E. J. Norris, 1885

Siegfried Tribolet, 1887

U.S. MARKET, VARIOUS LOCATIONS

Apollinar Bauer, 318 Fremont Street, 1879

Jacob Everhardy, corner 5th and Fremont Streets, 1881

RECIPE INDEX

ABOUT THE AUTHOR

Sherry Monahan is past president of Western Writers of America and holds memberships in the James Beard Foundation, the Authors Guild, Single Action Shooting Society, and the Wild West History Association. She has her own column and is a contributing editor for *True West* magazine and writes for *Cowboys and Indians* magazine. Other publications include *Mrs. Earp: The Wives & Lovers of the Earp Brothers*; *Frontier Fare*; *Tinsel, Tumbleweeds, and Star-Spangled Celebrations*; and *The Golden Elixir of the West*. Sherry also is a podcaster with various shows on What It Takes Radio. Learn more at sherrymonahan.com.